LET IT FLY WITH THE FLOWERS

A COLLECTION OF ESSAYS ABOUT THE INSTITUTE OF ECONOMICS, RANGOON, BURMA.

1/1/2015

EDITED BY KYI MAY KAUNG (PH.D.)

WORDS SOUNDS AND IMAGES

Also by K.M.Kaung

Novellas:

Band of Flesh and 53 Red Roses

ISBN 13:978-1507888629

ISBN 10: 1507888627

Black Rice

ISBN-13: 978-0615797526

ISBN-10: 0615797520

The Lovers

ISBN-13:978-1499193725

ISBN 10-1499193726

The Rider of Crocodiles

ISBN-13:978-1497498365

ISBN 10: 1497498368

FGM

ISBN-13: 978-1497497733

ISBN-10: 1497497736

Dancing like a Peacock & Koel Bird

ISBN-13: 978-1497514850

ISBN-10: 1497514851

No Crib for a Bed and Other Stories

ISBN-13: 9781499200751

ISBN—10:

Novel:

Wolf—upcoming

Poetry:

Pelted with Petals: The Burmese Poems

Intertext, AK, 1996

ISBN: 0-912767-15-4

Tibetan Tanka

Intertext, AK, 1996

ISBN: 0-912767-14-6

Words Sounds and Images.

KMKaung, ed. Let It fly with the Flowers: Essays about the Institute of Economics, Rangoon, Burma.

Rangoon University Convocation Hall—photo taken in 2014.

Burmese economists including Dr. Aye Hlaing, far left, and Dr. Maung Shein, center at either IMF or the World Bank, on right, U Htun Thin c. 1970s.

Sculpture of Dr. Aye Hlaing, Rangoon, 2014.

Rare photo from 1981, L to R, Daw Hnin Khaing, Dr. (then Daw) Kyi May Kaung, Dr. Khin Nyo Nyo. Photo by Maung Maung Hnyat, per kind favor of Khin Pwint Oo.

Dr. Hla Myint on his London School of Economics page.

Dr. Sean Turnell and Daw/Dr. Aung San Suu Kyi, c. 2014

Photo by Khin Pwint Oo--2014

Photo by Khin Pwint Oo, 2014

I like to paint in light and bright colors and dark colors and shadow as I think it is more true.

Zaw Win Pe

Visual Artist

Don't beat around the bush. Get to the point.

Dr. Aye Hlaing

Economist.

Just finished final edits.

Uploading tonight or tomorrow night.

Total is about 300 pages, but it is as tight as I could make it.

Thanks to all Contributors and Facilitators.

I give myself a bunch of flowers.

Actually, a friend took a bunch of red flowers to Saya Aye Hlaing's Memorial in November of last year, and with this we pay Tribute to all our Mentors, living as well as dead, and those we have never met such as Adam Smith, Arthur Lewis or John Maynard Keynes.

I just read that I never smiled while teaching the Economic History of Soviet Russia, and indeed, there was nothing to smile about.

There is a reason Economics is called The Dismal Science.

Kyi May Kaung (Ph.D.)

Facebook, June 18th, 2015.

TRIBUTE TO MY TEACHERS
BY DAW KHIN KHIN THEIN

To Sayas U HlaMyint, U Aye Hlaing, U Mg.Shein, Dr.Findlay,
Mr.Mali, Mr. Ray Billingsley, Mr Herceg . . . and all my Sayas and Sayamas

They were not mere academic mentors, dons

submerged in the abstract alone, ivory-tower academics,

amateurs acting out a charade of academic exercises

to a class of gaping, idolizing students—future leaders,

on outsize soap-boxes of the academic platform,

expounding problems abstruse, theoretical, mathematics-tinged,

niggling the intellect for the sake of mere intellectual exercise,

polemics, in the aerobics of the tongue;

but intrepid hunters for truth, optimal solutions

that chameleon-like can answer in many hues and voices

on the high gymnastic tightrope of intellectual honesty;

soldiers grappling to decipher unholy mesh of problems,

groping for practical solutions not only correct, but best-fit,

practicable, geared towards the future.

They taught us to be pragmatic, to look askance
upon the raft of cheap ready answers with a measure
of healthy skepticism, deliberation; principles
of both systematic thought, seasoned tools of analysis, reasoning;
fired in us intellectual curiosity, intellectual honesty,
not to mistake the well-dressed scarecrow for the human being—
mirage perplexing to the hilt, if sometimes convenient,
enticing; to deliberate the answer shy, elusive:
what should be…as what is,

as had mentors before them since Socrates, Hippocrates,
braving sacrifices personal and other, for their beliefs, values
based on conviction, dedication,
their true vocation.
Such were they, my teachers, dons, affording me
the exposure, pavilion, springboard for my intellectual progress,
career; theirs not the fault have I not shone like them,
despite their arraying for me as for all students, their stepping stones.

With respect and affection from their former student Khin Khin Thein

ENCOUNTER WITH TAKE OFF IN THE FORM OF AN ESCALATOR: ME AT THE LONDON SCHOOL OF ECONOMICS.

KHIN KHIN THEIN

Some people are experienced globetrotters which I was not at the age of twenty-one when I went abroad for my further studies.

The country I had been selected for was England and my College—the London School of Economics and Political Science.

Eager, fresh, like a butterfly newly out of its cocoon, I was journeying over a distance of approximately eight thousand miles on my own for the first time in my life.

Even before I had left Rangoon, I had never gone about on my own and did not know the traffic rules for pedestrians; it was therefore no wonder that when I came to the crowded streets and pavements of London, I really was lost and scared, not knowing where to turn, not knowing a single soul nearby either.

Yet even those first few difficult days of adjustments to a strange country had their moments of humor along with the pathos, though I did not realize it, always, at the time. It is of these funny aspects of my journey out, in spite of some inevitable harrowing moments, and of the first week of my arrival there, that I chiefly wish to relate here.

First there was the actual journey out.

Goodbyes were said and I stepped onto the plane, solemn, serious and completely void of feeling, whether of sadness, fear or excitement, and yet I was not really dead to the atmosphere round me then.

Then the plane took off and I looked out from my window at the geographical outline of Burma unfolding below as the plane rose higher and higher into the sky and was finally at a very high altitude.

I then saw the map of Burma as not just an outline on paper but as an actual fact. Still I felt nothing.

Then I gradually realized that we were nearing the outskirts of Burma and I felt a tightening in my chest.

Suddenly came an announcement over the plane that we had passed over Burma, and as suddenly, looking down at the familiar outline below, I was flooded with unexpected tears.

I felt anguish at leaving behind what I had always known, what comprised in a way myself; also, a journey all into the unknown for the fairly young and inexperienced is always harrowing.

There were three other Burmans on the plane all older than myself, but they were nowhere near me and I felt completely alone, and had a good cry for about half-an-hour.

The stewardesses were most sympathetic and soon I gained control of myself; also, 1 felt much better. I then took an unemotional, prosaic view of things, it is true, but at least I began to 'view' them again.

My journey unfurled on its amusing way.

First we landed at New Dehli for about twenty minutes.

I was still somber and subdued from the effects of the tearful outburst but I felt an interest in all that my fellow-travelers did and said in the air-port lounge.

Then we stopped at Teheran and Beirut.

Here my solemnity thawed and my Burmese fellow-travelers and I had orange juice and talked and laughed in the air-port lounge.

It was about eight-thirty then—I left Rangoon at five that evening, and as I looked around at the people and things in the lounge—bright lights, souvenirs, curios and curious people, I half-wondered that I should be there at all, among strangers, when normally I would be sitting down at home to a spot of study and work; I realized that the change had begun.

When we arrived in Baghdad, I was as alive and alert as the others, enough to inspect and select some souvenirs. I chose a bottle of perfume and a printed scarf, true to feminine habits. I began from then on to enjoy the amusing incidents that followed in the course of the journey.

The first such incident was at Frankfurt.

Instead of going into the lounge, we younger travelers strolled around the air-port. We came to a flight of stairs, quite stationary.

Naturally, we began to mount the stairs.

Imagine our horror, then, when without any warning, the stairs seemed to roll in or up or whatever you like to call it; the steps moved in, each under the other! The ground was moving right under our feet! Unused to such contraptions, we did not know how to stand straight, fell down and clutched wildly at the moving steps.

But of course, we could not clutch them.

They rolled ever inwards as it seemed, and we moved ever upwards, willy-nilly.

By the time the steps had moved inwards about twenty times, we were at the top of the stairs, much as we would have been had we walked up parallel flight of ordinary, steps, with just one slight difference: in the latter case we would reach the top in a standing position of dignity whereas we actually arrived onto the top landing literally on our hands and knees!

At least, two of us were half-way on our feet again, but a Thai girl simply refused to get up and off the stairs, though she was already at the top landing. She was afraid she might fall down again. The feeling of the ground running away with you can certainly do things to your stomach. We ourselves were red and laughing by this time with the exertion of energy, and coaxed her to let go of the stairs which she held on to for dear life. She seemed as though she was on the back of a runaway horse and was clinging on to its non-existent mane. Finally, our persuasive efforts and her own courage and sense of dignity triumphed.

She passed the first step of fear—that of standing up straight and taking the first steps forward, which had been a feat when she was a one-year-old and was a feat again now that she was thirty-odd. We sincerely congratulated her when she finally stepped onto the top landing where we were and she beamed as did we.

I for one felt amusingly like a veteran of the war.

This *Tawthuma,* some may say of me, but that was exactly what I was then in this respect as were the others and none of us were ever ashamed to admit it.

One does not measure a civilization merely by its contraptions or conveniences.

Also, how could we know and handle at once something we had never encountered at home? and why should we mourn the absence of such things at home when they are merely fruits of and not aids to progress? Such things-

"moving stairs" as I had written home and which I had heard of before, were called "escalators".

So much for the escalator.

The only point about it was that all of us youngsters knew that this was only the *petit hors-d'oeuvre* preceding the vistas of new things that we were yet to see.

So we moved on.

*

Our next and final stop was London. Together with three other Burmese travelers, I got off the plane for good. The only Burmese man among us guided us through the customs and then we were through. Then we noticed people who came to greet us—our "welcome committees"

My "welcome committee'' was a Burmese student who had been my Saya in my second year in college and his Burmese friend.

He had been requested by the Burmese Embassy in London to meet me. Neither of us recognized the other, so changed were we both.

However, the Burman with me noticed them, asked them the right questions and then introduced us.

Then, putting me in their capable hands, he brushed me off his own capable hands and went away with a sense of "duty done".

It was rather amusing.

*

We departed from the airport and went to the Burmese Embassy to report my arrival.

The "Chancellor" there remarked of me "she's very tired; she's slightly in a daze'', as I really was though I didn't know it before then. The fatigue of travelling twenty seven hours straight was telling on me, not to mention the effects of the emotional outburst that graced my departure from Burma. "Go to the Alien Registration Office to report. You will receive a card that registers you as a temporary citizen in England. Then go eat something, and go home and rest" was the advice that I heard from the tired depths of my mind.

I had not slept on the plane and now I was beginning to droop.

So off we went to legalize my stay in England.

There I was given a little green booklet complete with my particulars and a nice fat number attached to my name.

I understood then what aliens feel when they registered as Foreigners.

The card seemed to shout at one, "You are a second class citizen: you are not of this country". The number something like DF 005398 made me feel like a convict.

Needless to say it was an entirely new feeling.

The feeling was not so much because of the number but because I was told that I must always carry it around and that I was liable to be arrested at any time if, when required upon for any reason to do so, I could not produce the card.

It was an awful feeling.

Actually it was only because I was new that I felt like that, for later on I learnt to regard it with less awe.

I grew quite neglectful of it as I should not, renewing it sometimes weeks after it expired. 1 was able to do this only because they took a lenient view of students there and I met with nothing but kindness and helpfulness everywhere.

Then my Saya-cum-fellow-student asked me whether I would like something to eat.

I felt both too shy and *ah-na-de* to keep them longer and also as all I wanted was sleep, I said no.

I however bought a large bun and was then seen to my hotel.

There the Embassy had booked me a room for two nights until I could be admitted to Crosby Hall, a famous Hall of residence for University women professors, post-graduate students, authors, journalists, poets, artists, etc.

Crosby Hall was alright, but the experience of two nights in a strange hotel was both frightening and amusing.

There I was in the hotel, in the topmost room above five tortuous flights of stairs completely enveloped in darkness. There were light-switches on the landings but I was too ignorant of the fact, and too frightened even if I knew it to grope around for them and switch them on.

The first time, my Saya saw me up there with my suitcases which he carried up, there being no lift (or elevator), refusing my help.

Having thus installed me in my abode, he left to keep an appointment, with a friend.

Then I found that I needed something badly, I forget what it was.

The dismay I felt!

I went down, raced down was more correct, in the darkness, and asked the landlady where I could get such and such a thing.

Again, I felt too shy to ask her about the lights. Following her instructions, I found little difficulty in finding my way to a Boot's chemist shop.

When I tried to retrace my steps however, reversing her instructions mentally, I found I was in trouble.

I found myself going in a full circle twice or thrice round a block of buildings.

Night was falling, street lamps began to glow, and I was ready to burst into tears, overgrown baby that I was.

Reminiscent of what Tennyson had said in his "The Charge of the Light Brigade", there were buildings in front of me, buildings behind me, buildings to the left of me, buildings to the right of me, but for the life of me, I was as perplexed as could be, and could not distinguish one from the other; all were blocks of buildings, all uniform grey in colour, height and width, all rather ugly to look at, all surrounded by the same angular roads and pavements, allowing only a glimpse of a patch of blue sky above.

In short all seemed to be identical.

Where were the landmarks I had noted in my mind as I came along? Now, two to three hundred lights blazed in the form of house-lights, shop-lights, street--lights, car-lights, lights from big advertisement hoardings, all heralding the night.

Swallowed up somewhere in this general assembly of lights were some lighted signs that I'd used for landmarks. I had never expected this.

Now I seemed to be in the middle of a fair and did not know in which direction my 'home' was. It was frightening. I almost panicked but that was only for a moment. Knowing that no panicking could help me and that if only I was sensible, help could be around, I looked around for a person whom I could ask. Recognizing a police-officer, I went across to him.

He was about six-foot four in height, I was only five; the traffic din was growing.

To hear, therefore, he almost doubled up in bending down, so it seemed to me, placed his ear at the disposal of my voice and told me to repeat my question.

This whole performance rather disconcerted me, however there was no help for it, and I reiterated my query.

It was as well, for he showed me how to get back to my place. According to his instructions, it was so easy!

Even so, rather doubtfully, I traced my steps according to his instructions and found myself outside a fairly familiar block.

Almost holding my breath, I looked around at the number plate of the building, and let it out thankfully again, how thankfully I shall never be able to tell.

It was my place.

Even then I did not dare believe my good-luck.

I pressed the bell, and only when the door swung open to reveal the kindly old lady behind it did I know I had come to safety and a haven at last.

Sometimes, it is not the comfort and luxury of a dwelling, but it's plain, wholesome security that is Heaven.

*

Once inside, my terror was over, but not completely so were my troubles.

I switched on the first landing light under the old lady's supervision and went up the stairs with dignity as befitted a young Burmese lady.

However, when she had disappeared into her own suite of rooms, and the landing light went out which was most unexpected, the young Burmese lady was speeding up the stairs in steps of twos and threes, aided in her speed by a childhood fear of the dark.

I had never before been away from home alone and it was most frightening for me to be so now in a strange world in the dark.

Moreover, as I raced up, I almost ran into a man on the landing just below me.

I had never been acquainted with alcohol before, but I was not dumb enough not to recognize that he was reeking of perhaps whisky.

Startled, I rushed up the stairs even more swiftly.

Once in my room, having locked my door, I looked down below from my window upon the endless stream of traffic, lights winking, people briskly and busily passing on their way, and waited to get back my breath.

Then I was calm and almost happy.

However, when unexpectedly there was a sharp knock at my door, I jumped up rather scared. "Who's there?" I quavered courageously.

"It's only me, dear" said a woman's voice.

"Who's me?" I persisted.

"—from the Burmese Embassy".

"Oh!!!"

I felt a warm rush of gladness and flew to open the door.

I then saw a portly elderly lady there looking like a benevolent fairy god-mother, just when I had been wishing to hear a friendly Burmese voice.

I could have given her a thousand hugs there and then.

She had come to see that I was alright, and the gratitude for that thoughtfulness that I felt, I cannot describe.

It was a lot to me.

She waited around chatting while I munched the remainder of my bun, unpacked, repacked and generally moved around.

When she left, I no longer felt either frightened or sickeningly alone.

Though I thanked her shyly just once, in my heart were a thousand thanks.

*

By the next morning when I woke up alive and well, I decided that I would be alright in this country for the rest or my stay in it.

Still I did not wish to stay longer in that hotel, eerie as it seemed to me, and so I was most pleased when Crosby Hall took me in a day earlier than expected and my Saya came to see me there.

Once again, I was glad, for at Crosby Hall we met some Burmese lady doctors who were some twelve to thirteen years my seniors and to whom I took an instant liking.

The problem of a few people to guide me a bit in the city and of Burmese company for me was solved.

My Saya, with a thankfulness that equaled only mine, passed me over to these ladies all but physically, saying over my head, to my chagrin: 'She's very young (meaning immature) and only twenty years old and also all alone. Please look after her."

The lady nodded and so for the first few months of my arrival in England, I was under her capable and protective wings.

*

Two or three days later, I went to LSE (as the London School of Economics was called in short) with two English girls who were also going to attend a course of study there, and tried to memorize the way for two days or so.

From then on, I was utterly on my own so far as going to and fro the School was concerned.

The School was about three to four miles away from Crosby Hall and there was no direct route either, by bus or by train, there.

Naturally, it was hard going at first, and I made mistakes in taking trains (called "tube'' there) and buses.

I had to learn a lot in a most alarming manner sometimes.

However, people were always most kind and helpful, and I always corrected my mistakes speedily. Never did I learn so well the truth of the English proverb 'All's well that ends well" as when I arrived, safe always, at my intended destination, after having first chugged away in opposite directions. Yes, learning to find my way amidst difficulty taught me the spirit of independence, and self-reliance to a fair extent.

LSE turned out to be a group of three enormous, grey buildings joined together by bridges on all the third floors.

There were separate common rooms for staff, post-graduates and undergraduates and as many different restaurants and cafeterias there.

There were facilities for tennis, squash, badminton, football, etc., much as we have here, and a large, room for quiet relaxation.

I was pleased with all this.

Besides this, the library facilities there astounded and delighted me, the conditions of study under constant electric light in the grey rooms rather dismayed me, and I was disappointed by the lack of grounds and landscaping and gardens that LSE had.

I had been spoilt by the lovely Rangoon University campus.

Students here should realize they are lucky in this aspect—in fact, I'm sure they do, in their own way.

I even told some English LSE friends of mine that whereas we have beautiful acres of land at home for our University campus, the only bit of ground that LSE seemed (at first glance) to own was in the flower-pots on its terraced roof.

After that laugh with them, I felt better, also, knowing that it was not what was outside, but inside the school that mattered most, I settled myself to working with a will and with pleasure.

Thus, my life as a fully-fledged student in England unfolded, and as it turned out, I became extremely fond of LSE in spite of its austere appearance.

I retain very happy memories of it, despite a few bitter ones there.

All in all, I was a lucky Burmese student.

Yes, I am glad that I journeyed there.

Khin Khin Thein

October 13, 2014.

REMINISCENCES OF MY SAYAS AND SAYAMAS

BY

THYNN THYNN WYN

Today, my old colleague Khin Pwint Oo and I had a nice chat on the phone, and we talked about the open call for the Institute's Golden Jubilee tribute.

She suggested that I think back to our days as students and the time we spent with our teachers while studying at the Institute.

She has bright ideas but I am afraid I don't.

She encouraged me to drop her a few lines and so I send back these few thoughts that came immediately to mind.

*

There are many teachers for whom I have great respect but I am sorry I cannot write about them. Why?

The trouble is I cannot collect my memories back.

From among them here are a few sayas and sayamas, whom I would like to thank.

The first person I would like to remember is Daw Kyi May Kaung.

She taught Economic History to us in our undergraduate year.

I admire her because unlike others she does not seem to talk much and she always talks softly, but she is very much familiar with her subject.

Out of the things I remember most from the lectures she gave us was about the Meiji Reforms in Japan. These were the famous Reforms which brought Japan into the modern world.

I and my two friends always went early to her lectures and we never missed her class. It was as if we were listening to the story of Meiji of that time.

She is intelligent, so she could relate almost everything about the Meiji period, and I think she did not leave out anything, including things like culture and politics and even dress codes, sword-making and the Samurai and Daimyo systems.

She became my Master's thesis supervisor and I was so happy that she was to be my supervisor because she is the one I admire secretly. But I was afraid to talk to her because she is so full of knowledge and I am not bright like her.

She was quick at reviewing. When I submitted a chapter to her in the morning by the afternoon she gave me back my file to me with all the comments in detail. She was not only concerned about my written thesis but also concerned that my viva voce (orals exams) went smoothly.

She was like a mother who worried about her daughter.

All Master's theses at the Institute had to be taken up to the English Department for final English grammar editing, but the Head of Department, Saya Leonard Kangyi, told me that I can take it back.

His comment was, "it is perfect and I believe that I do not have to do any more editing on your Supervisor's stuff". That means she is good in the English language too.

Another thing that I would like to share is about Professor Maung Shein or U Shein.

He was about to leave the Economics Department and his Economics Students to work at a U.N. agency overseas. I was a student majoring in P.D. (Planning and Development).

What I want to say about him is his style was so affectionate and genuine. He came into the class and he started saying "What I wanted to talk about for today is—" then no words came out of his mouth for quite a long time.[i]

He kept scratching his head, with his right hand scratching the left side of his head and then moving his left hand reaching the right hand side of his head and then went on repeating like that.

We students looked at each other and we were so amused to see him at a loss for words.

But I still remember him well with his examples in class, especially when he gave lectures on Population Boom. He used to ask "Do you know why poor families have more children?" The answer he gave was clear. "It is because they have no other entertainment like rich families, so they have nothing to do but to go to bed telling each other *pone-to-pat-sa* (the story of this and that) and then they have all those *pone-to-pat-sa* coming out one after another." [ii]

I remember what my friend KPO who suggested I write this article (she is senior to me) once told me about another of Saya Shein's famous in class examples. It was on giving a clear cut example of the disparity between rich and poor. What he said was—"Suppose we are thinking of our children's education and we want our children to become doctors (a very popular career choice in Burma).

"And let us assume we have two families, one is rich and another is poor. Even if the student from a poor family has the same in-born talent as the child of a rich family, the latter will become a medical doctor, and the one from the poor family will become only a *bein-daw-saya*(traditional medical-practitioner), meaning that the son of a poor man cannot be brought up to become like a rich man's son, though he or she may have the same innate ability.

The classes I was in with Rector U Aye Hlaing were so frightening.[iii]

It was not just I.

Everyone was scared of Saya.

One day he brought a bundle of books but not a bundle of joys for us with his office assistant Ko Kyaw Sein, carrying another bundle walking in behind him.

Once he sat down in his chair he started to throw books one after another to each of us randomly and said that he will ask questions next week on what we have read.

*

The day arrived.

I tried to hide myself behind my classmate sitting next to me.

She is fat so I thought I would be all right to avoid seeing Saya U Aye Hlaing, but I was called out to give my review.

It went tumbling over.

After the class my friends said if you look straight into him he will not ask you, but when he saw you hide like that it made him ask you - no doubt.

Never try to hide next time.

So that was the lesson for me.

*

One more memory concerns Dr Myo Nyunt and U Myat Thein.

Students used to call them Bo Myo and Bo Myat because they were so close to their students.

What made me remember on Dr Myo Nyunt was –he would ask us to go to Librarian Daw Hlaing Hlaing Cho to get what he (Dr Myo Nyunt) had recommended. The names of each of us was listed with the books (new books not even registered yet with the library) for us to read.

With U Myat Thein, the thing I cannot forget is whenever he uttered words and he needed to be diplomatic (at that time it was not allowed to give comments freely) he would joke "Well, mind you students, this is not what I say, and never let your tongues slip when you happen to go out talking with others. Leave those words here—that means in the Class."

These are the little memories I can so far recall to take part in contributing for the Golden Jubilee of our alma mater.

Thynn Thynn Wynn

October, 2014.

TRAVELS IN THE DELTA

BY KHIN PWINT OO.

I plug my MP4 into my ear and at once the River Road song comes on.

Here I go once again. With my suitcase in my hand, I am running away down river road.

Since I changed my career from working in the university to working on field projects, I am traveling all the time.

Now I am heading out to the Lower Irrawaddy Delta Region.

Without travelling in boats throughout the townships and beyond, I would not be able to relate to life in delta grass-roots communities.

As soon as I got my appointment letter from the Project, I packed up my things in a suitcase and started off to a place with which I was not familiar, but I was eager to go anyway.

*

It was in a cold December in 1999.

I had to take a boat which was run by the Inland Water Transport Company.

It was a double-decker, tightly packed with passengers and loads of cargo.

The boat usually departed in the early morning from Rangoon, traveled all day long, winding in and out along the waterways, and finally arriving at its destination in the evening about six o'clock.

I had never been to such a town.

All I had with me was the address of the field office.

Upon arriving, I looked for a taxi to place my belongings on.

I could not find a taxi, but only a trishaw or a tricycle, pedaled by a man.

The trishaw driver took me to the address I showed him.

As is usual he tried to take me the long way so he could ask for more money.

The town I went to is one of the river towns in the evolving delta community, and the chosen township where I work on a community development program.

In a few days of my arrival in the Delta, I looked for an opportunity to take another boat trip.

I was excited to take a boat ride out in the wide river on a locally built outboard motor boat, though not a big one. It could accommodate about fifteen passengers and their luggage.

This was the beginning of my life in a rural community in the Delta region. It is quite different from my earlier on-farm visits as a university student and tutor. Previously, I had only traveled in the Dry Zone of Central Burma.

My first funny episode was in stepping down from the boat onto the landing stage, which was a home-made wooden bridge with planks tied to posts.

I did not know how to step from the boat onto the pontoon so I first tried to wade in the water by the bank, without taking off my rubber thonged footwear (what my Sayama Kyi May calls flip-flops) to prevent myself from stepping onto substances that I could not see underneath the water.

The water was just knee-deep, so I walked with slow steps, but my feet got stuck in the mud and I could not lift them.

A boatman had to help me.

I was welcomed with mirth by the villagers when I got onto the landing stage, because my legs looked as though I had long black rubber boots on.

I too could not stop myself from laughing.

Except for those village elites, ordinary people from the village were simple and helpful.

They assumed that the coming of project staff was to help solve their deprivation, as though we were gods when seen through the eyes of these people in the rural communities.

One of my duties was to travel to project villages that were situated down river, near its mouth, in an adjacent township.

It was a real shock to me.

I never thought that I would go there.

The day I traveled it was raining but not too heavily.

I ventured out in a small boat this time.

Unfortunately we ran into a rainstorm on the way.

The boat I was in was rocking up and down on the waves, as if I was on a gigantic roller coaster.

I tried murmuring the words of the *sambuddhay* prayer, asking for the Buddha's protection, but my teeth were chattering.

One day my office staff and I had to go for a follow-up monitoring visit that was in a part of the township close to the sea.

It was a place well-known for its crocodiles.

The village was called the Nest of Crocodiles.

It was a nice trip, the weather was fine and the air so pure, and the food we had for that day was also delicious, crabs and prawns which were expensive in the city.

I forgot to think about those ferocious crocodiles.

Luckily, we did not find any crocodiles, though we heard stories about people and draft animals like cows dragged away by crocodiles.

We delayed leaving.

On the way back, one of the ears of the propeller attached outside the boat broke when it hit something hard under water.

We could not go on, as much as we wanted to, and so by the time we reached the town it was almost 11 o'clock—dim and dark in the night. The town folk had gone to sleep and there was no one to be seen on the streets but only the three of us—my assistant who accompanied me, the boat driver, and me.

There were only a few street dogs that welcomed us with barks from the roadside lean-to huts.

Once I was taken to a medical practitioner or *Say Saya* in the words of the villagers.

It was in one village where I happened to stay for the night.

I ate a nice evening meal with foods I had not eaten before, and I got into trouble—food poisoning—late at night.

The villagers were so worried that I finally gave my consent that I would go to see the doctor.

There I was given an IV shot, and I did not even have the strength to ask what he injected.

In a short while, I somehow felt better, so I came back to my host's house, stayed overnight and the next morning I went off to see the doctor to thank him, and to tell him I was leaving the village.

We were to move to another village, and as we traveled in a boat my assistant asked me how I felt.

She told me that the Saya who gave me the intravenous shot was not a real doctor, but a *wet-saya,* a vet who inoculated animals such as pigs, chickens, or cattle.

So he was not even a quack or a local medical practitioner with no *sa-ma*—i.e. a person not holding a medical license to practice.

*

I ran into bare-foot doctors or back-pack medical attendants while I was doing my field assignments in the Dry Zone.

They were a husband and a wife team. The man had served as a *hsei hmu* or a person in charge of a military medical corps. His wife was a traditional birth attendant or *le-thè,* not a trained midwife, going from one to another village.

One day, I suffered from a toothache, and my host said she wished the bare foot doctor would come, he used to come every alternate month to the village.

She encouraged me by saying that once I was given an analgesic shot, I would be alright and she added "That medicine man is a nice person who will not charge you much".

Villages quite far from town still have to rely on these back-pack medical attendants.

Another unforgettable day was when I came back from my field trip in a boat with a bigger engine.

There were only two of us, my boatman and me. On the way we ran into a sudden heavy rain and squall, the sky was dark and cloudy and we could hardly see the way. We were almost nearing the town and in the next ten or fifteen minutes we would arrive in port so I decided to take a risk, although maybe I should not have. I had no other option but to assist the boat driver, looking out to see if there were any other small rowing boats going and coming our way.

I was concerned to not miss the next day's meeting in Yangon.

It really was a hard time for us because we were traveling on a river where the under currents that flow were not the same, meaning that one under-current could be flowing in a north and south direction, while another was going in an east-west direction.

Our boat almost capsized because of these cross currents.

My boat driver managed somehow and was quite skillful.

The crew from another anchored boat we passed by on our way back was surprised to know nothing happened to us, and that we were still alive.

I became a helpful person in a different society, having to learn to know the people who deserved support.

I had to find the ones who were struggling, living hand to mouth and vulnerable, and assist them.

I found many.

One was an old woman who was living all alone in her little shabby house in a coconut plantation site. She had only one son, who had been working in the salt industry as a piece-rate laborer. He could not come back often to see his mother as his workplace was not in his village.

The old woman was in her late nineties. The neighbors brought her a food, but only sometimes could they share. So she was provided monthly basic needs, mainly rice.

It is so heartening to run into another two-member family—a poor mother and her son who was blind. The project gave them a small rowing boat. She and her son sold groceries in their vicinity, using that boat. I helped her son by giving him a white-cane, which I find is useful to a blind person like him.

Another pitiful story was about a group of women. There was a scheme where the project supported self-help groups to earn a living through IGA or income generation activity. The activity the group decided on was to transport crabs to the local wholesaler in town. The crabs have to reach the towns very early in the morning, to fetch a good price.

However, luck was not with them. Not long after they started this business, the boat they loaded crab containers capsized.

The people on board all drowned in a whirlpool.

*

Life is very uncertain in the Delta Region.

I feel content to have an opportunity totally different from that of my previous experience as an academic.

I may not be able to get this irreplaceable moment of life to contribute to humankind if I had not taken this assignment on community development.

So, this is my life, a life of true inspiration.

*

Biography of Khin Pwint Oo

Khin Pwint Oo has lived in Yangon since birth.

She received her Bachelors' Degree in Economics, majoring in Agricultural Economics and a Masters in Economics, Yangon, and a Masters in Development Studies, Western Australia.

She works in different capacities as a field-researcher, working in collaboration with the Institute—where she learned and earned as an academic; as a field project staff officer, as the United Nation's National UNV-Volunteer in different UN Field Projects and Missions; and on short-assignments abroad.

Her experience in the field has led her to Community Development Programs in her home country.

Currently, she undertakes project assignments as a freelance consultant.

THOSE WERE THE DAYS

BY SINTHEINGIE

If my memory is correct, it was in 1964 that we attended our final year B.A (Hons.) Economics class at the Institute of Economics in Rangoon.

By 'we' I mean the sixteen of us, four women and twelve men.

Our lecturers were Dr. Aye Hlaing, Dr. Mg Shein, Dr. Ronald Findlay, U Tha Hto, Dr. Than Nyunt, Daw Khin Lay and Dr. Khin Nyo Nyo.

At that time, we were unaware of how lucky we were to have such educated and well-qualified and experienced teachers.

Our teachers had different teaching styles:

Dr. Aye Hlaing would usually quicken the pace of his lecture should any chatting and whispering occur.

This worked well. The noises stopped at once.

Dr. Findlay lectured, holding a piece of paper and a piece of chalk. I remember his remark on the birth of his daughter— holding up a hefty text book by J.A Schumpeter, he said "This book weighs as much as my baby, eight pounds."

Dr. Than Nyun's style was to walk to and fro across the stage, tossing and catching again a piece of chalk.

Dr. Mg Shein would be so engrossed in writing on the blackboard that he at times almost stumbled to the floor from the stage.

Daw Khin Lay taught with such a sweet voice.
However, any interruption would evoke a disdainful stare from her.

Dr. Khin Nyo Nyo was always stylishly dressed, and was never ruffled by any interruption whatsoever.

U Than Hto would occasionally raise his eyes to the ceiling during lectures.
I remember that when we became tutors in the Economics department, Saya would occasionally remark that an academic atmosphere
was absolutely necessary in the institutions of higher learning.
That is, faculty members should have ample time to read and pursue their respective academic disciplines to further enhance their learning.

At the end of their lectures, our teachers usually gave us long reference lists, causing us to rush to the library to grab the books
before others got them.
There were sometimes squabbles over the books.

However, once out of the library, our quarrels were forgotten as we crossed over Inya Road to the Inya Lake at the back of our Institute.
At that time there were no institute compound (grounds) barriers as at present,

we were free to roam around the lake areas.

We would first feed ourselves fried gourd and other deep fried Myanmar snacks at the small

shops.

We would then head towards the boat rental, rent two boats and row abreast in the lake, singing songs, pulling each other's legs--figuratively, of course.

This was our daily routine.

Sometimes we would roam the RASU-Rangoon Arts and Science University campus, and then heading for the student centre, play badminton. Then sometimes, on special days such as the Kachin State Day, Chin State Day, etc....we gorged ourselves at the Kachin food stall, Chin food stall ..

In addition, there were sporting events, hall dinners that we enjoyed so much.

Ah! those were the days, those memorable, unforgettable days.

Sintheingie

Department of Economics

October 2014

A MYANMAR ECONOMIST I KNOW AND ADMIRE

BY

MA MYO NWE

Daw Khin Nyo Nyo (we call her Ma Ma Nyo) is an outstanding Myanmar Economist I know whom I have admired a long time.

She is now eighty seven years old, but still going strong, and sharing her time with her old students whenever she can.

She was born on September 1927 and she is the youngest of the four children.

Her native town is Shwebo, a town notable because of the famous King Alaungmintayargyi (U Aung Zeya), also known as Alaunghpaya in the history of Myanmar.

As a child she was given in the primary and middle schools at St. Joseph's Convent, in Mandalay (once a *Min: Naypyitaw,* which was a Royal City in BE[iv] 1221).

She continued her high school studies at Wesley Girls High School in the same city Mandalay, until the great World War II broke out in 1940. Thus, she was matriculated only after the war.

She continued her further study in Rangoon University and obtained the Bachelor of Commerce (B.Com) Degree in 1951-52. At about the same time, she was offered a job as a tutor in the newly opened Economics Department of the University College of Mandalay.

After some years, she was sent abroad under TCA Fellowship to work for further studies.

In 1954, she left for Madison, Wisconsin, USA and was conferred Masters in Economics Degree from the University of Wisconsin, USA.

When she came back to Mandalay she was promoted to a position of Assistant Lecturer in Economics in the same department of the Mandalay University College.

For some years, Mandalay University College had been planning to become a full-fledged University. No doubt, its Economics Department also needed to be fully equipped with technically better trained personnel. For that, she was given another chance as a Colombo Plan Trainee to go abroad to pursue her Ph.D. degree. She was selected for University of Toronto, Toronto, Canada.

Her subject is Financial Economics and she obtained her doctorate in 1962.

When the Institute of Economics was founded in 1964, a group from Economics Department, of Mandalay University was transferred to Yangon, automatically becoming staff members of the Economics Department of the newly established Institute, the Institute of Economics in Yangon.

There she was promoted to Lecturer, where she worked steadily until she retired in 1988.

While still in service, she wrote books on International Trade and that is mainly prepared for the Economics students, as a guide book.

She continued writing many articles, mostly on globalization and development.

Well-known articles are All about Globalization, and The Economics of Development, that were published in *myet hmauk ye yar* (Current Affairs) Magazine, in August 2006.

She kept writing articles and did translations, up until 2008-2009; and her renowned articles *Gaba mjei hpjan kje la chin: gjaun pjaun: le: la ya mji. Gaba achei anei mj:*[v]was published in July 2008, and the translated was published in October 2009. *article Si:bwa: jei: let hpjaun. thana' thama: ta u: i. wun khan che' mya*

She is now living contentedly with her family. She and her husband U Maung Maung Kyaw, a retired Director General of the Ministry of Trade, and her only daughter and son-in-law live at her residence on Than Lwin Road, Kamayut Township, Yangon.

Ma Myo Nwe

October 2014.

Biography of Ma Myo Nwe

Ma Myo Nwe obtained her Masters in Economics, from the Institute of Economics, Yangon.

She worked as a Tutor in Economics Department, Institute of Economics, for 12 years from May 1971- March 1983.

Then, in the same year, she moved to Foreign Economic Relations Department, under the Ministry of Planning and Finance, in Yangon [later the name of the Ministry has become Ministry of National Planning and Economic Development]. She worked there for 27 years, initially in the Staff Officer Post. She became Assistant Director in 1989, Deputy Director in 1996, Director in 1997, and Deputy Director General in 2003. Soon after a year she became Director General at the same department, until she retired from her position in 2010.

During her years with the FERD, she served as ASEAN Senior Economic Official for Myanmar from 2004-2010; Alternate Governor for The World Bank and ADB; as National Coordinator for Economic Cooperation Program, GMS: Greater Mekong Sub-region; Steering Member of ASEAN Mekong Basin Economic Cooperation Program; and also a Steering Committee Member for UNDP/IHLCA Project.

After her retirement, she took an assignment as a National Consultant, in UNDP/Integrated Household Living Condition Assessment Project, for about a year until 2012, taking the full responsibility in tasks such as preparing survey instruments, monitoring price surveys, and price data validation.

NOTE TO THE RARE PHOTO, BY KYI MAY KAUNG

I did not go to get my degree in person for either my BA Gen. Hons in Economics, nor for my MA, and I wish I had.

I did go to get my Ph.D. in person in a stadium in Philadelphia in May 1994, where a famous conductor, then with the Philadelphia Orchestra, Ricardo Muti, gave the opening address.

I remember him saying, "I am always conducting with my back to the audience, so it feels strange standing facing you."

It was boiling hot, much hotter than Rangoon. Most of the American students were wearing shorts under their gowns.

I was with my former classmate Joyce, who also recd her Ph.D. She was born in the Virgin Islands and was also a Fulbright in India.

Anyway, this photo says it was taken in 1981.

We were probably in the robing chamber to the right, waiting for the ceremony to begin.

To my right is Daw Hnin Khaing, a great friend of mine, also family friend, also good in both English and Economics. She planned an "English text" for Economics Institute students based on quotations from Keynes etc.

She was the wife of U Stanley Cho who worked at BOC (The Burma Oil Company) and was the son of my father's best friend U Cho. She was also the sister-in-law of Ma Ma Helen Cho in the Eco. Inst Library.

On my L is Dr Khin Nyo Nyo--(Ma Ma or Elder Sister Nyo).

She was my office roommate for about five years after I was appointed a lecturer.

She told me many useful things, such as the language requirements in doctoral programs in the USA, how big Philadelphia was, and lent me a copy of Walpola Rahula, *What the Buddha Taught*, and looked after me a lot, even once waiting for me to drive off in my car (perhaps after this ceremony), before leaving in her own car.

Thank you, Ma Ma Nyo and Sawthandar Kyaw (Ma Ma Nyo's daughter).

Thanks Khin Pwint Oo for this photo.

All our offices on the third floor burned down in 1982.

I have five degrees—one BA, two MAs and one Ph.D.

I have written several books and won several prizes.

KMKaung

4-29-2015

Facebook

A SHORT INTERCHANGE WITH DR. MYO NYUNT[vi]

Dear KPO, Kyi May,

How do we in Myanmar create a progressive Rural Society, Economy and Structure (Instititions) to achieve Sustainable Livelihood for rural village people trapped in permanent poverty and underdevelopment. I really would like you and others, with a lot of relevant grounded experience in our country to forge and design a framework and approach to achieve Sustainable Economic Development of The Myanmar Economy. When I returned to Myanmar for the first time in 2012, I broached the subject with certain friends and individuals but was warned that "outsiders" were still not welcome in Myanmar. Anyway with all the work that has been done during the last two decades plus and recently the rush into Myanmar by concerned States, groups and individuals to assist in "the making and reforming of Myanmar polity and economy" I think, my two *pyas* worth that the "time has arrived" for some of us to propose alternative approaches to social and economic development at local-community level in Myanmar.

Arriving 30th Oct, to listen and observe. Planning to visit Magwe, Pauukhaung, Salingyi, and Myaing. Also have been invited to participate in a Workshop to be held in Mandalay.

Definitely will base it on your work at Yadaw

With Metta Bo Myo.

Unlike · 1

KMK: It will be "sustainable" when they stop skimming so much off the top.

From Facebook, October 2014.

ANOTHER FACEBOOK DIALOGUE WITH DR. MYO NYUNT–

U Myo Nyunt: Nowadays after fifty years being tagged as a doctor of philosophy—economics, economics, still reading studying and trying to understand The PHILOSOPHY of Life and political economy of change in and of my country of birth and always belonging—But always to others a *ma noo ma nat* (half-cooked) Burmese failed economist.

With Respect. Myo Nyunt. Rangoon University (1954-59).

Kyi May Kaung: U Myo Nyunt, don't worry about the opinions of others—how well-cooked do you think they are? They just make their living by saying what the junta/NGOs want. What is so great about that?

Myo Nyunt: I agree Kyi May, I just posted trying to correct certain misconceptions on FB about senior civil servants like your father and U San Lin, who were public intellectuals and men of character—civil (civic?)virtues. So much angst—Kyi May, that's what I cannot stomach. Not that I myself have not veered towards errors and omissions in my life. With Metta. Sayar Myo.

Unlike · 1·

KMK: I've got to the age where I do not care what people think, one way or the other. I know who my friends are. As for the rest, they never liked me anyway, and so they can shove it. I never liked a lot of people I was thrown with due to circumstances either. I just don't want you or anyone else to go away thinking they are "failures."

U Myo Nyunt: No Kyi May—always I appreciate and honor their achievements, they showed the Way, that you, I travel on. Success-failure to me is all results measured by our own instruments and values, properties/attributes we consider as important. With Metta. Sayar.

KMK: We are talking about two different groups of people—

FaceBook 3-22-2015

MEMORIES OF MY MENTOR DR. BO LAY

BY DR. KHIN SAW NYEIN.

"There's no shortage of topics that you can write about."

That's what my mentor, Dr.Bo Lay told us when we were at the beginning of the term of our final year(fourth year). As submitting a term-paper was one of the requirements to get our bachelor degree in economics, many of us were worried because we had no idea what to write about. The academic year was 1967-68 and at that time we could not check out term-papers written by old students; therefore, many of us had very little idea of what to write about or how to write a term-paper. One day, during his lecture, Dr. Bo Lay asked us about our term-paper topics and when he found out that many students had not even chosen a topic yet, then he said the above words and added, "You will never run out of topics to write until you die." I did not understand the full meaning of his words then, but as I grew older and gained more knowledge and experiences, I came to realize how right Sayar was.

Dr. Bo Lay had the ability to simplify and make a difficult topic easy to understand. We Planning and Development major students had him only in our final year and he taught us Econometrics, Perspective Planning and Manpower

Planning. Econometrics is a relatively difficult subject involving economic theory, statistics, and mathematics but due to Sayar's systematic style of teaching we were able to follow his lectures; he would state the topic, define the terms, write down the main points, explain the steps, state the essence of a topic, and make criticism and analysis.

I remember Sayar drawing two vertical lines on the blackboard(we didn't have white boards then) dividing it into three segments so that the main points and equations that he wrote down would not get mixed up. Thanks to Sayar, we had the chance to study not only theories but also applications; his assignments on econometrics were based on real data for the Burmese economy. We had to do tons of calculations manually (we did not have electronic calculators back then except for the ancient manual ones in the Statistics lab), so Sayar's assignments honed our math skills a lot.

One of Dr.Bo Lay's contributions to the Economics Department was compiling, translating, and publishing lecture notes on econometrics, and manpower planning. While he was acting as the president of the Economics Association, several issues of Economic Journal were published, and some of the articles in those issues were used as references. There was a publication titled Economic Development and all the articles, including Schultz's and Becker's theories on human capital and investments made in education, were translated and compiled by Dr. Bo Lay. In addition to teaching, Sayar had also carried out several research projects on the Burmese economy using econometric models, and some of his papers were presented at Research Forums.

While Dr. Bo Lay was still working as a lecturer at the Economics Department, he was appointed as Deputy Minister of the Ministry of Co-operatives and later worked for the Ministry of Forestry in the same position so Sayar had fulfilled his duties as a citizen by not only imparting his knowledge and experiences to the students but also applying them for the good of our country's economy.

More than twenty years had gone by since Dr. Bo Lay had passed away but I believe his sharp intellect, keen mind, and clear thinking had left positive impact on those who had closely worked with him.

Khin Saw Nyein

August 23, 2014

MEMORIES OF INSTITUTE OF ECONOMICS, RANGOON.

BY TIN HTA NU

I first worked in the Institute of Economics as a research assistant under Professor of Research, Dr Khin Maung Kyi. I took part in collecting survey data which I learned a lot from the late Professor Dr Khin Maung Kyi and Saya Dr Myo Nyunt. These were valuable experiences which I later used for my research overseas, especially Saya Myo's methods of probing, noting and observation in farm household surveys.

I joined the Department of Economics as a tutor Headed by Saya U Tha Hto in 1973. After being appointed, we were sent to Central People's Services Training in Phaung Gyi. All new tutors from Economics, Statistics and Commerce departments appointed in our batch had to attend. We had a very good camaraderie among us as we had to go through the hardships of the training. The Phaung Gyi friends, Daw Lei Lei Yu and Daw Tin Tin Yu from Statistics Department, Daw Nwe Nwe Lin and Daw Khin Soe Thu from Commerce Department became my lifelong good friends.

*

When I started working, I shared Room 117 with other tutors. Most of them were my teachers when I was an under graduate. The room had two compartments. The first one held four senior tutors who were my Ama Gyis (Elder Sisters)—Daw Aye Yi, Daw Sein Sein Yee, Daw Nyunt Nyunt Yin and Daw Khin Htwe Than.

I knew all of them well before I became a staff member, as I sometimes visited Daw Nyunt Nyunt Yin (Ma Ma Mie) whom I had known since I was a child. In the second room were Daw Tin Hla Kyi, Daw Sin Theingi, Daw Khin Sandar, Daw Thit Thit Lwin, Daw Mi Mi Gyi, Dr Khin Saw Nyien and myself. All of them welcomed and guided me in my new post. We were very cohesive, and had good working and social relationships, like a big family.

I felt our room 117 seemed like a hub of our department, and we have extended family members like Daw Khin Thein Yee, Daw Khin Khin Thein, Daw Hla Kyu, Daw Hla Than, Daw Khin May Yee and U Than Swe.

*

For teaching, I was assigned to tutor in the Economics of Socialism and Modern Economic History. The students called the staff who taught these subjects "Modern" Sayama/Saya or "Social" Sayama/Saya.

In those days, being modest was the value of society, so neither being social nor modern was appropriate. The title was a joke among us young tutors.

When correspondence classes started in the late seventies, we had to go and teach economics at other colleges and universities as well as broadcasting some topics. We had to teach in the regional colleges during the Institute's term breaks.

Saya U Tha Hto was very kind (he must also have had a lot of headaches) in letting us choose the colleges we wanted to go and teach at. We were always arguing among ourselves who wants to go with who, where, and to which college or university. I often travelled with Daw Khin Sandar and Daw Mi Mi Gyi. We had to find our way among different campuses for teaching and residing in colleges that were not familiar to us. However, we also had many good times exploring the region after our teaching duties were done.

When we were all back from teaching we had a great time giving each other little gifts from the region: Mandalay *htoe moant*, Myitkyina *khaw boke*, Shan *chin* from Taunggyi.

I really missed that later when I was teaching in Australia. Nobody here gives anything to colleagues wherever one goes.

*

After Saya U Tha Hto retired, our Head of Deparment was Dr Than Nyun. In 1981, Professor Dr. Than Nyun informed tutors who did not have Masters degrees that they could apply for scholarships to Australia. My dear very kind teacher, friend, and neighbor Professor Daw Khin Lay (Ma Ma Lily)[vii] encouraged me to apply for a scholarship under the Colombo Plan to study in Australia. Together with a few other staff and my best friend Ma Ma Joan (Daw Tin Hla

Kyi), we were selected to go and study in Australia. Four of us were to study at University of New England, Armidale, New South Wales.

I did my post graduate degrees majoring in Agriculture and Resource Economics in 1982-84.

Whoever came back from overseas had to give a seminar on our experiences and what we had learned or researched. I presented one of the projects I did on a Resource Planning subject. It was based on one of our trips to teach those correspondence courses. Together with Ma Ma Sandar and Ma Ma Mie, I went to teach students in a correspondence course. After our work, we went sightseeing to Inle Lake. I was told by one of our friends who took us there that the lake's water level is being reduced as the floating fields used up some land and water. I had an idea on the resource use, so I put it in as a project in the resource use planning subject. It was the MAUT (Multiple Attribute Utility Theory) where tourism, agriculture and fisheries competed for the usage of the lake. In my project, I put some priority attributes and weighing scales among the three industries.

I found that tourism is the most favorable for the local people with agriculture and fisheries as second and third industries to focus on.

I was later assigned to teach Agricultural Economics by the late Professor Daw Khin Lay.

I had a lot of job satisfaction as I could redistribute the knowledge I had acquired in Australia. Also under her supervision I had the chance to carry out some surveys. The highlight of my career in IER was when my teacher, mentor and Akogyi (Elder Brother) Professor U Myat Thein assigned me to assist him in the Kinda Watershed Management Project. The experience my colleagues and I had in data collection for household surveys through narrow hilly parts of Ywa Ngan district on foot carrying our information papers was very valuable.

The farmers practiced slash and burn agricultural practices and were encouraged to plant trees for maintaining the watershed area for Kinda Dam.

The farmers' participation rate in growing trees was low as they could not sacrifice their land for long term crops, thus facing loss of income. They perceived their sacrifice was for city people downstream to get regular electricity through Kinda Dam and not for them. One farmer gave me an insight into urban bias planning through his angry remark. He said that the famers in their region and the cities downstream are like two brothers inheriting a cow. As it is not practical for the long term to kill the cow, the two brothers agreed to take own half of the cow each. The elder brother had the front part and the younger brother got the back part of the cow. The elder brother feeds the cow, but the younger brother gets the milk and cow manure.

The upland farmers are thus elder brothers who grow trees that give no immediate return but generate electricity for the benefit of downstream people. The consumer-producer negative externality affected the behavior of upland farmers.

This conversation with the farmer gave me a lesson that I could apply in my lectures and research in participatory planning, as well as on managing projects in Asia and the Pacific. In addition, I even use this farmers' example in the regional area I live in now. I create awareness at local councils to avoid urban-biased policies in implementing our region's development.

I left the Institute of Economics in 1990 to take the position of an instructor in Assumption University in Bangkok, thanks to my teacher Daw Tin Tin Aye (Ma Ma Peggy).

I must say I do admire Ma Ma Peggy's fair and systematic management of the staff of the Business Economics Department at Assumption University. Several of my former colleagues and friends from IER were also working there, so we had a small Economics group. Daw Su Su Tint and Daw Nwe Nwe Yee (Ma Ma Annie) from Statistics, Daw Myat Mon from the Commerce Department and Daw Yu Yu Hlaing from the Economics Department were also in our group.

In Bangkok, the academic environment was still like Rangoon, expatriate academics could still be in their comfort zones. The beautiful Burmese culture of teacher-student and teacher–teacher relationships was still in the air at Assumption University. We helped each other at work, and also with many Burmese students. Apart from academic work, we also had extra curriculum activities such as celebrating the Thingyan water festival and Thadingyut, the festival of lights. I left my colleagues from Assumption University a year later to work in the University of New England (UNE) in Australia.

*

Now in my retirement reflecting on work experiences, I can say my days at the Institute of Economics Rangoon (IER) have made me who I am.

The guidance provided by ethical teachers at IER will never leave me. Giving time for the students' academic needs; guiding in all aspects; standing by in their crises were all prevalent in my teachers at IER.

At UNE, I was warned by my senior colleagues not to give too much time for students, but told to be selfish and do more research publications so that my career as an academic can be successful.

I did compromise by presenting research papers but to involve and guide the students' needs is a difficult task in Western academia. I recollect some points what my teachers have guided me, and have used in my career. They all have taught me in many ways, however, I would like to express some excerpts and my applications.

Professor Daw Khin Lay: Try to do research on sustainable land use. Yes, Ma Ma Lily, although I did not finish, I attempted my Ph.D. research on organic (sustainable practices) and mainstream (chemical using) farming practices and have given seminars.

Professor U Tha Hto: Look into the efficiency of the farm with its productivity. Yes, Saya, I tried to use this concept in feasibility studies in projects I worked in Asia and Pacific.

*

Rector and Professor Saya U Myat Thein: My present as a parting gift before you leave is this Kinda Watershed Management Project. Yes, my dear teacher and *akogyi*—I have used in many ways as case studies, conference papers, lectures and comparative studies in promoting people's participation in projects.

As our culture instructs, teaching is a noble profession. I respect all my teachers with this article. I also send *metta* to my friends and colleagues.

Tin Hta Nu

Bio:

Tin Hta Nu started her career as a research assistant in 1970-73, appointed as a Tutor in 1973 and worked as Assistant Lecturer from 1985-1990 at the Institute of Economics, Yangon.

She went abroad and re-started her career in academia, as a Demonstrator, at Assumption University, Bangkok in 1990-1991; moved to Australia where she worked as Senior Tutor and Lecturer at the University of New England, from 1991-1998. She took an International Consultant assignment from 1998-2002.

In 2003, she established a Farm, determined to work on organic farming and educating local people on sustainable food production.

She worked as a Tutor, in Camden Haven Community and Adult Education College since 2004 until the present.

She also works in different capacities—with Kendall Community Hall as Trustee, since 2008; Co-Founder in Mid North Coast Refugee Support Group since 2012; Agriculture and Environment Officer, Country Women Association since 2011; Coordinator, Community Garden, Kendall since 2011; Co-Founder, Community Café and Farmer's Market since 2005; Volunteer, Community Co-op-shop since 2004; Project Coordinator, Kendall-Kadaw Friendship School Project since 2005; Project Coordinator of Thukhita-Yama Nunnery in Yangon for orphans since 2012.

She was chosen for a candidature for the Greens Political Party at the Local Government Level, and became a candidate in 2010. All her work in the Kendall and Camden Haven Regions is still going on, inspiring her and she is also a free lance writer.

STRUGGLES WITH BUTHI-NGABAUNG-KYAW

BY YEE MAY KAUNG

To visit Japan without knowing the language can be a real disadvantage, but learning Japanese can be quite an ordeal, too.

Before I went to Japan, I had only studied Japanese grammar and the two sets of syllabaries[viii], Hiragana and Katakana. I had almost no idea of the intricacies of Kanji—the ideographs of Chinese origin which we Burmese sometimes jokingly call *buthi-ngabaung-kyaw* because of the many strokes in each character, in writing: They look like our gourd fritters called *buthi-ngabaung kyaw*.

The Japanese use these characters together with the two sets of syllabaries.

To say the least, this is extremely confusing.

When writing these characters, the number of strokes, their relative lengths and the order in which the strokes are written is of all importance.

Usually, I would put in one stroke too many, or too short or too long.

But the worst obstacle, by far, is trying to read these characters.

None of them have a fixed unique reading, but a number of them, sometimes as many as ten or more for a single ideograph, and when to pronounce how is the problem.

As the standard vocabulary consists of around two thousand characters, one can imagine the size of the problem.

As for using a character dictionary, it needs a lot of perseverance and memory.

In our language school, it was the students from the Peoples Republic of China, Taiwan, Singapore or those of Chinese descent who had a great advantage over us. In their case, the problem was first to unlearn the Chinese pronunciation of the characters as most of the Japanese characters (about 90%) are the same as those the Chinese use.

It has been said that a Chinese person and a Japanese can make themselves understood merely by passing notes to each other with ideographs on them.

But most of us in the elementary classes in frustration would just read by inserting "Kanji" whenever we came across a Kanji character in reading.

Efforts towards Romanization have met with considerable resistance because many identical-sounding characters have completely different writings and the meaning of a sentence cannot be construed from the context alone.

One needs to see the ideograph to understand a sentence properly.

After my initial struggles with these, I came to regard them as the very essence of the Japanese language.

The meaning also became easier to remember once we understood its origin.

For instance, the character for "tears" combines the characters for a door and a dog crawling under, while that for "self includes the ideograph for "nose"; the Japanese, when speaking of themselves, usually point at their noses, rather than at their chests, as we do.

The character for "easy" combines a roof and a woman under it.

This can be taken exception to by the Women's Lib movement, I suppose.

The teachers at the language school must have had a hard time with a new batch of students every six months and all from so many different countries. Each nationality had its own difficulty with pronouncing certain sounds; some couldn't pronounce, "tsu", others mixed up "sh" and "ch" and still others could not say the "kyu" sound. Moreover the teachers just could not teach us to write from top to bottom in columns and from right to left. It may be added here that there are a number of things which are just the reverse of what we are used to doing—no doubt, the Japanese must believe that we do just their reverse, and find it funny also!

For instance, books are opened from the back; rice is eaten at the end of a meal—this is supposed to clean the palate. In addressing people, the appropriate form of address, such as Mr., Professor, Teacher or Dr., comes after the name.

I am sure I must have offended a number of people by forgetting to put in one of these forms after their names when speaking to them.

A pleasant way to learn Japanese is when riding on the subway railway because of the recorded (sometimes live) announcements concerning the next station, available train connections and other information, and also because of the colorful advertisements containing beautifully written ideographs and adorned with glossy photographs. As commuting takes up a large part of the time of modern Japanese, most of them have learnt to read or sleep (or knit and crochet in the case of women) either standing or sitting in the carriages.

For foreigners, though, the advertisements were very attractive and kept us from falling asleep; we did not dare fall asleep in case we missed our stations.

With Japan's ever growing international role, the Japanese language now has an increasing number of foreign words, usually transliterated into Katakana. These are sometimes a far cry from the original word because there are no sounds for the union of two consonants. Thus "noodles" becomes "noodoru", "fruits" becomes "furootsu", and "Bridgestone (tyres)" becomes "Burijisuton".

One word in a subway advertisement which puzzled me for a long time was "su cheemu basu". The advertisement showed a smiling man with a towel round his neck. I would mutter to myself this word frequently (one can usually discover the original word by saying a katakana word very fast, several times) wondering what it could be. When I finally realized what it meant I felt as if I had made a major discovery—the word meant "steam bath".

All in all, after nearly two years of Japanese, my English and Burmese have deteriorated while my Japanese is not as fluent as I would wish; in fact, I now seem to be in the process of slowly forgetting what I have learnt through lack of use.

ON THE SUBWAY

I used the Osaka Subway so much that I know it much better than I know the Osaka which lies above the ground. At first, since all the signs in the subway were in Japanese, I had to memorize my way to the language school, feeling rather as a "rat-in-a-maze-experiment" must feel, or maybe a blind mole in its underground tunnels.

Going to school was a routine something like this: I went down into the underground station, stood in line with others at one of the marked places where the doors of the arriving train's carriages were going to be opened, got on, got off, changed to another line and then got out of an exit which also had to be memorized.

At rush hours, it is usually every man for himself; for all that it is said that Japanese are one of the most polite people in the world, you should see them at rush hours in the train (or at department store discount sales) where you will be elbowed out of the way or have your toes stepped upon without compunction and no apologies either.

In the underground stations the people just stream along like so many ants in an ant hill. The need for pushers at rush hours to push people into the already packed carriages really shocked me. But who can blame them if they compete so hard—imagine a hundred million people on a few small islands—of course, they must compete to survive.

Male chauvinism is always evident when riding on the subway, or any other means of transport. Many times I have been pushed out of the way by a Japanese male eager to reach an empty seat first. One of my classmates, a Singaporean, came to our seminar in a huff, one day.

He told me that as he was riding on the bus that morning he saw a young lady carrying a baby and some heavy shopping bags, so he got up gallantly to give her a seat, only to have the seat taken promptly by the young lady's husband! He was so angry, he nearly told the man to get up and give him back his seat, but then, he thought it better not to. It is a very common sight to see the women carrying very heavy loads plus babies strapped on their backs, while the men just carry a book or newspaper. Still, each culture has its own rules and who are we to make judgments?

The old and the handicapped are very independent. Very old hunched-back men and women can be seen using the subway without any companions. (Quite young children, too, seem to be so disciplined that they do not need to be accompanied by adults.) The handicapped in wheelchairs can get on and off quite easily. Similarly, the blind can use a special pavement with raised cobbles, by feeling it with their sticks. (Traffic lights are also equipped with a short recorded tune, to indicate the green light, for the blind). There was a deaf-and-dumb school near one of the stations on the way to school and many of the students would get on at the station and would "speak" in sign language at a very fast rate. They always fascinated me but I could never understand what they were talking about. They were always so full of life and seemed to laugh a lot in spite of their silent worlds.

Japan today could aptly be called the land of vending machines. Vending machines are everywhere especially in the big cities. From hamburgers, milk, soft drinks, beer, coffee and tea to cigarettes, magazines and comics (porn and otherwise), all of these can be got out of a vending machine if you have the right coins. Of course, there are machines to change your currency notes into coins and naturally, machines to change your coins into other appropriate coins. It is all very efficient and impersonal. Except that sometimes your change does not come out—if this happens at the station ticket vending machine, you have to press a button and a face appears at a little window (which shows there is still some use for the human being). You have to say (if you can manage it in Japanese) that the machine has not given back your change. If you cannot, it is better to let your change go, rather than miss your train. Sometimes, too much change comes out in which case it is better to go away quickly.

The subway system is almost completely automated. Ticket collection is also automated at most stations. Going in, one has to pass a row of wickets operated by light beams; the ticket is put in and it pops out already punched. It has to be kept and used at the exit station wicket. Some of us lost or threw away the tickets and had to pay fines up to three times the ticket's value. If the amount of the ticket bought is too low for the distance covered, alarm bells start to ring when you put your ticket in the exit wicket. This is a most embarrassing situation because everyone looks at you as if you were a thief. The bells ring mistakenly also and that takes some explaining too.

A number of ways to beat the system exist and have been handed down from each batch of foreign students to the next but to use them one needs a lot of nerve. I did try using them but gave up quite early due to lack of nerve.

OF CHOPSTICKS, NOODLES, AND ME

As everyone knows, the principal eating device in Japan is chopsticks. They could be called a patience-testing device. I never have been able to understand how the reputedly short-tempered Chinese have been able to put up with them, let alone invent them. Chopsticks are also an exquisite torturing device to make one eat as small a quantity of delicious food as possible in a given period of time because one just cannot get the food into one's mouth. I know from experience that it can thus be used for reducing weight, having tried them in chasing some grains of rice on my plate. This leads me to the theory that perhaps, chopsticks were invented because food was so scarce in China.

The first few months after I arrived in Osaka, I would watch enviously the Japanese eating fried chicken, very adroitly tearing off the flesh from the bones with chopsticks. To me, being able to eat fried chicken with chopsticks seemed to be the height of proficiency and I aimed to be able to do the same eventually (without sending the chicken halfway across the room) especially as it became very irritating to have my Japanese acquaintances trying, in a condescending "there's-nothing-to-it" manner, to teach me how to use chopsticks. (I, on my part, used to think they had terrible table manners, being very noisy in eating, smacking their lips, slurping their soup and even drinking soup straight from the rim of the bowl).

Actually the secret of eating with chopsticks lies not just in the handling of the chopsticks but also in having appropriately "cut up" food. All Japanese food is cut up into small morsels, or rolled as with rice balls, which can conveniently be picked up with chopsticks. The rice is also a rather sticky kind and can be quite easily picked up in lumps. In the case of dishes with sauces or gravy, only the solid pieces would be eaten and the gravy left behind, a waste, but there is a lot of waste in Japan now, as the people become more and more able to afford it. Food left over in restaurants will seldom be packed and taken home.

I always thought that it was only the Chinese who love noodles and consume it in large quantities. But no, I found that the Japanese love it, too, and have even invented some other forms of noodles such as large flat noodles, small flat noodles and buckwheat flour noodles. This last kind has a brownish-purplish color and to me always looked extremely poisonous, maybe because I usually associated purple with poison from looking at pictures of deadly nightshade when I was a child.

In addition to these, there is the noodle to top all noodles, a sort of symbol of development—this is the Cup Noodle (known as Kappu Noodoru in Japanese) or Instant Noodles in dehydrated form with bits of dried meat, spice and stock powder in a paper cup, plastic wrapped, ideal for misers and midnight larder raiders. All it needs is boiling water to make it edible. It can even be obtained at the universal vending machine on street corners, in which case all that is needed is the suitable number of coins and pressing the machine button –the machine adds the hot water automatically.

The ability to eat noodles with chopsticks is a good test of skill, especially boiled noodles in soup which are all knotted together. It seems not to be good manners to cut up noodles into shorter pieces; could this be because noodles are sometimes a symbol of longevity? I tried classifying noodle eaters and came up with three types. The first is the Noodle Novice who has never eaten noodles with chopsticks before. He can be identified by the way he holds the chopsticks—one in each hand. He will carefully wind the noodles round each chopstick like thread and tip the chopsticks so that the whole bunch of noodles will go sliding into his mouth. The Cautious Noodle Eater might slowly stir and stir the noodles around as if waiting for the noodles to get cooler but in fact he never eats at all but just pretends to. This class usually consists of women too who do not know how to use chopsticks and do not like to risk looking foolish. The Perfect Noodle Eater can eat boiled noodles without spilling a drop of soup. They can also handle chopsticks perfectly and are to be envied for the way they eat their noodles so elegantly. Their technique is to cool the noodles by lifting them out of the bowl with chopsticks and gently blowing; they just bite off a bit of noodles cut off the whole knot, (or suck up the noodles) and drink a little soup every now and then. I think the best way to eat noodles with chopsticks would be to copy the method of one "Kyant-Ba-Hone", a great detective in a comic strip, who used his chopsticks to knit a muffler and then ate the muffler. A very neat solution, the only difficulty being that I do not know how to knit.

Yee May Kaung

COMPARING MENTORS

BY KYI MAY KAUNG

I have been reading what my colleagues at the Institute of Economics, Rangoon, wrote about their experiences, and I am indeed surprised that their mentors told them such specific things to study and come back with.

Mine never did, even with respect to some earth-shaking events that would change my life.

For instance, when I was about to get married, I marched into Saya Aye Hlaing's office and said "I am getting married."

Saya sort of grunted--"So long as you finish your MA. In one year, not two."

*

For my Master's topic, Dr. Findlay did suggest I look into Project Appraisal and go to the Railway Department (where my Uncle U Shwe Shane was Chief Engineer) and get data to compare steam and electric engines. He also suggested looking at the Polish shadow interest rate and showed me how it was just an interest rate with the usual present value/recoupment formula.

They never said anything specific, but of course I was formed intellectually a good deal by working with them.

I will never forget Saya Aye Hlaing's lectures on the Economic History of Burma and the World, his rather hands off "supervising" of my translations for two textbooks, the many times he sent me running downstairs to look up specific things for him, such as a two tier exchange rate.

Of course this was while he was Rector, and before he was appointed Union Bank Chairman.

And I remember the money circulation amount he said kept him awake at night.

When he had to stop his Applied Economics lectures, due to pressure from the government (junta), I almost died.

But I decided even though he could not teach it openly anymore, I would keep my own ears and eyes open.

*

From Dr. Findlay, I also learned "hands off" supervision. He told me—"write it that way, you know what I mean," and so I wrote it on paper begged from the university press downstairs, and delivered it before I went on maternity leave.

From Saya Findlay, I learned that "a true gem will not get smothered in mud" from the very real racial discrimination that he went through, all during the period when he was stuck in a small room, and had only me as a student, being denied the position of department chairman.

Later, in Poland and in America, I continued to study the Problems of Communism, which he had first made me aware of by his classes on Soviet Planning Experiences.

In the United States, Burma Expert Dr. Josef Silverstein was my external examiner for the doctorate, and always strongly supported my thesis.

All Soviet expert Herbert Levine suggested was, why don't I learn Mandarin. I wish I had.

Systems expert Henry Teune and later my Ph.D. Committee Chair just looked up my thesis title with one click, and said, "It hasn't been done yet. Do it. It is going to be a bestseller."

Later, he lost one copy of my dissertation on a flight somewhere in the pocket of the airline seat in front of him. But I had been well advised by all my friends and classmates never to give anyone my only copy of anything, and always to give all my supervisors the same chapters at the same time, so it was not a disaster, as Elizabeth Bishop said about Loss.

I can't be like the sword eater who denied his mentor the heron, and got the sword stuck in his throat.

Truly I have been fortunate, and some colleagues have even, with one word or sentence, guided me about my offsprings' education, or like Saya Khin Maung Kyi, praised me for doing well.

In life, one meets a lot of fools and jealous manipulative people, but none of my mentors has kept a closed fist.

Now he is gone, I can say it, but Saya Aye Hlaing even had me edit the other professors' English and had me edit his Ph.D. dissertation, all while I was still a student.

Thank you.

*

A few years ago Saya Findlay steered me to a professor at Columbia University so I could help her find panelists for a conference on the Rohingya in 2012.

I did not even know he gave her my name.

Life is very strange.

*

When Ma Ma Jane (Mrs. Findlay) and Saya left Burma, I could not bring myself to say goodbye, and then we all met up again.

Kyi May Kaung

6-8-2015

MY MEMORIES OF SAYARGYI DR. AYE HLAING

BY DR. KHIN SAW NYEIN

My Sayarma Ma Ma Kyi May (Dr. Kyi May Kaung) mentioned that Sayargyi U Aye Hlaing as “the kindest of humans” and I totally agree with that statement.

Although I did not have the opportunity of studying under Sayargyi U Aye Hlaing for a long time, I had personally experienced his kindness and concern.

Soon after I got my tutorship in December,1964, an examination for selecting candidates for state scholarships was held, and I was lucky enough to pass it.

At the farewell party for those who were going abroad for further studies, Sayargyi mentioned an Assistant Lecturer who went abroad as a state scholar, got married to a citizen of that country where she was studying, and did not return to Burma.

Sayargyi said that this young Sayarma was a simple person but I was simpler than her, so he was worried that I might follow in the same footsteps. I was about twenty three or twenty four at that time.

I'm glad that I did not disappoint him.

When I was studying at the Moscow State University for my Ph.D., U Tin Htut from the Commerce Department came to Moscow on a short study tour together with two other officials from other Ministries.

Sayar U Tin Htut took the trouble to come and visit me and check on me whether everything was fine.[ix] He told me that Sayargyi U Aye Hlaing asked him specifically to visit me to see if I was OK.

I felt so thankful for his concern.

It was only about four years ago that my own father had passed away, and I was only in my mid-twenties at that time; being in a far away foreign land with only a few Burmese, I felt downhearted sometimes, and this caring gesture of Sayargyi quite overwhelmed me.

It gave me heart to study harder so that I could successfully return with a Ph.D. in hand.

Another example of the caring nature of Sayargyi for his staff was when I got engaged; I invited Sayargyi U Aye Hlaing and Professors of Economics Department. Sayargyi U Tha Hto and his spouse Ma Ma Myint came to my engagement. Sayargyi U Tha Hto told me that Sayargyi U Aye Hlaing asked him to attend the occasion as he himself could not come. I'm not sure whether he was hospitalized or had other important businesses.

I suppose he was glad that I did not get attached to a Russian or any other foreigner, came back and was about to marry a Burmese.

As a young tutor I was afraid to approach Sayargyi U Aye Hlaing at first, but after I had seen his kindly and caring nature I came to look upon him as a father figure. Khin Saw Nyein, 2014.

MY MEMORIES AS A STUDENT AT THE INSTITUTE OF ECONOMICS

BY MA PWINT (A.E STUDENT OF 1973)

I still plainly remember my days as a student as though it were yesterday.

After graduating from high school we had to make three choices based on the marks we achieved, to apply to university.

I was finally selected to join IOE, although it was not my first choice.

The very first year of my university life seemed like a release for me, since I was the sort of person who loves to live free.

It was quite good that I did not have to be in a nutshell, to sit in a four walled classroom the whole day like in our high school days. What a delight. A huge campus so cool, lush and green to roam about in, and the view of the Inya Lake close by, that is so spectacular.

To have different lectures given by different lecturers at different times, and to have a wide circle of new friends.

I and my friends from my high school days got separated. They got into other Institutes like the Institute of Medicine or the Institute of Technology or some came to RASU, The Rangoon Arts and Science University.

Though it was a bit unusual to be a freshman, and to look for friends, I found I could easily make friends with my classmates in the Accountancy class, who were like me with the title Ms. Know Nothing about Accountancy.

I cannot fail to recall those days in my freshman year, especially, when a light cool breeze across Inya Lake crept into Theatre 10 (where we had our Accountancy class) that gave us students a nice afternoon catnap.

English, Burmese and Geography were my favorites. I did them well in each. I was especially good at drawing maps, contours, graphs and charts that I was acknowledged by the tutor in the Geography practical workshop. As a freshman student, it did not enter my head to be a bright student, but rather to enjoy a full life in my first year at university.

When I became a sophomore [second year student], I was quite used to life as a co-ed. I do long for my cronies, as we used to skip classes together. Now, we are all separated.

The new friends I met in my second year came from all over the country and had different backgrounds, socially, culturally and financially. I went to the Students Recreation Center to play badminton or hung around the History Department in RASU across the road, went to the Judson (Church) Student Center, where my friends were taking music classes on the Burmese harp.

Nevertheless, I tried not to miss lectures in Economics, especially the Economic Analysis class where the lecture given by Daw Khin Khin Thein, aroused my interest with interesting things to learn in Economics.

I was poor in mathematics and accounting subjects. I was summoned by the Head of Department of the Commerce Department Daw Hla Hla Aung, for getting grade 1.0 in Costing in the first term test.

I was told to get grade 3.0 at least, or I would have to spend another sophomore year.

Despite that, I was able to catch up. I must admit that without the special class given by U Aung Tun Thet, who was a tutor at that time, but now, an Adviser to the President, on Costing, it would have been definitely a difficult year.

In looking back at my life as a third year student I realize that my grades in my sophomore year excluded me from majors in the Commerce field for my third year of study.

I did not feel bad.

I happily said goodbye to Accountancy, and Costing, the boring subjects for me. Without any hesitation I made up my mind to enroll in a program majoring in Agricultural Economics. I knew I do not need to shoulder those subjects I was not good at, and could go into subjects I was interested in, I would do well.

I got to know the others because we were only thirteen students [there were only four female students] in my third year class.

We had one who was a good artist; another in composing poetry; a chubby lad in clowning; we had an athlete; a book-worm; a body builder; and me a jack-of-all-trades.

It was also a good experience to know the lecturers closely as it was a small close knit class, different from my first two years of college.

The very first person to got to know was Dr. Myo Nyunt, who walked into class. We noticed he was an unusual person who wore black-rimmed thick eye-glasses, and a *paso* or sarong that he wore almost pulled right up to his knee. Without weighty books in hand he was not a complete man. He introduced himself, telling us his name and the subject he is going to teach us; then came another . . . and another, and finally we students got acquainted with all the lecturers who would be with us the whole year round.

Though I did not know what it really meants, we were told by senior AE students to keep *Hto-Lay-Myo* in our minds.

Later I learned that *hto* meant U Tha Hto (Head and Professor of the Department) who was going to give lecture on Agriculture Policy, *lay* meant Daw Khin Lay (affectionately called *daung-ma-lay,* by the students, for she looked like a dancing pea-hen, when tucking her *pa-wah*[x] at her back—she looked like a feathery-winged pea-hen) who was a senior lecturer in subjects such as Farm Management, Agricultural Statistics, and Econometrics/Quantitative Methods. And *myo* was Dr Myo Nyunt, who lectured us on Agricultural Economics.

So, that meant, we students could not get away from them as long as we were majoring in A.E.: Agricultural Economics.

It was a real joy to have lively lessons on Agricultural Finance with Dr. Khin Nyo Nyo, whom students in the 1970s called "Daisy Nyo," because she always looked as fresh as a daisy, always well-groomed.

After a few weeks of study with Dr. Myo Nyunt, we were buried under his assignments. They were a lot for us, to look for references in the IOE's library or to run to the University bookshop to fetch books on Economics written by Paul Samuelson, Baumol and H.Myint. We students had to sacrifice our pocket-money to buy those books.

We dared not the sharp eyes of Daw Khin Lay, during her lecture class on Agricultural Statistics, and so also with Professor U Tha Hto while he was giving his lecture.

We were afraid to be absent from class, because there were only thirteen of us in class and it was obvious who was missing.

After a year of study, the term ended and I did come out with pretty good grades and the thirst of knowledge in A.E. subjects carried me on to maintain good grades in my next year of study. We continued to study under the same professor and lecturers in our final year.

I felt I chose the right subject. Majoring in Agricultural Economics was the right choice. I did not have to go for field visits to villages, but I came out with grades that qualified me to proceed to the Masters' Class. My parents were delighted. I was not the bright one amongst the three children of my mother. She told me that she never thought I would even finish my high school, for I spent two years each in my ninth standard and tenth standard classes.

My friends, after graduating, started to look for jobs, but I, and also my classmate, remained at the IOE, to continue my education. Masters' class, Part I, was tough, because, subjects in Mathematics, Social and Economic Statistics, and Economic History for me were real hurdles.

Mathematics was taught by the Head of the Mathematics Department, U Hla Myint. As I am pretty bad in Mathematics, I had to struggle with calculus and matrix algebra; I became a two-time-outstanding student, *nha-htut-kun Lu Ye Chun,* and had to spend two academic years in Master's Part I, because of the extraordinarily poor marks I got in Mathematics. The next year I passed with grade C.

Dr Aye Hlaing was, then, the Rector of IOE; but he also gave Masters' classes lecturing in Social and Economic Statistics. Students hardly missed his classes, because once you did so; you would have trouble catching up. We all had to be alert during his class, all ears to his questions. If you answered him back with irrelevant points, you would get a smash from him, "*You better go ask a trishaw-peddler for that answer*".

He was a candid person, but kind at heart on his subordinates and students. Fortunately, I got grade A- in his subject.

Another subject Masters students had to be serious about was Economic History taught by Daw Kyi May Kaung. She later became my Master's Thesis Supervisor. She was a well-read person, and we students hardly ever saw her smile.

She brought with her a few books in hand when she came into the classroom. Then she would place them on the table, but she, without glancing at the pages, would talk straight away on the subject matter as though she had swallowed all the words in those books.

The subject itself is difficult, requiring wide reading (and to name a few, we had to put our heads into the economic history of Soviet Russia, those Bolsheviks and Mensheviks, and to memorize the Russian names "skys" like Trotsky, for instance) and you could not expect a good grade.

The lecturer in History would not give you a good score unless you were able to articulate your thoughts well. I came out with C+ for that subject, not a good grade.

My Master's Part II was fine, mainly because I did not have anything that had Mathematics in it, and the other subjects were quite relaxing for me because there were no classes to attend, the time was up to you to go on with your own pace of studying . . . reading text books, searching references of relevance, discussing with your mentors on subject matter and submitting assignment papers.

To my surprise, I stood first in class, in order of merit; that I received an appreciation from my Professors and Lecturers.

All in all, my university life as n Economics student was really enlivening, even though there are subjects that made me bored and bothered me.

That is natural for we live a life of pros and cons in every single thing we do; but normally, the cons are more bumpy than the pros, so the best way is to cherish your years while in university, because you cannot get that experience twice in your lifetime.

Khin Pwint Oo

Nov. 2014.

KMKaung, ed. Let It fly with the Flowers: Essays about the Institute of Economics, Rangoon, Burma.

MEMORIES OF DR. AYE HLAING

BY MAUNG PYE AUNG (U HLA HPYU CHIT)

I sometimes think that the days before my time at the Institute of Economics might be better.

All my teachers looked very professional, academic, smart and happy.

Even then, I have come to the conclusion that my days at the Institute were my "Golden Age"—academically at least.

I wish to give examples for this statement: Please look at our teachers and the faculties and our library.

Just to name a few of our Professors, we had very well known Professors with brilliant academic achievements: Dr. U Aye Hlaing (Rector), Dr. U Shein, U Tha Hto, Saya William Paw, Dr. Khin Maung Nyunt, Dr. Khin Maung Kyi (and I should add also my teachers like Dr. Bo Lay and Dr. Myint Tin who were senior lecturers at my time but I see them more as Professors too as I listened to their lectures which were very clear, and after their classed the students really learned something).

*

There was another famous Professor too when I was a student at our school, Dr. Ronald Findlay, Professor of Research.[xi] We usually saw him together with Dr. Khin Maung Kyi, who was Professor of Management.

Dr. Findlay did not teach us, but whenever I browsed the books at the library,[xii] I could see his name at the back of the book among the list of borrowers of the book. In 1995, together with my friend and colleague Dr. Maung Maung Lwin, we paid a visit to his office at Columbia University in New York City.

My under-graduate years, 1965 to 1969, came and went quickly.

In my first year, we were taught all major subjects: Economics, Statistics and Commerce (in particular Accountancy).

I had to struggle very hard with accountancy although my lecturers were Daw Yi Yi Myint and Daw Po Po Khin who were very good teachers.

My tutors were U Than Tun (Ashok Nath) and U Roland Khin and they were also very good and I think because of their tutorials and teachings I passed accountancy. I still remember one incident though. After the accountancy final exam, I was so worried whether I would pass or not. As soon as I was out of the exam room, I saw one teacher going out of our school towards the canteen. I quickly followed him and called him from behind. He turned and looked at me with surprise, as he did not know me. I asked him, if I did not pass accountancy what would happen to me. He smiled sympathetically and replied "don't you worry young boy—you will pass."

He looked as if he had predictive powers and I believed him.

He was Dr Bo Lay.[xiii]

I passed my first year and in the second year I took the combination of Economics and Statistics and "out of danger" – Accountancy.

Starting from my third year I took Planning and Development as my specialization. Dr. Bo Lay taught us Econometrics in the fourth year which I graduated with distinctions in Econometrics among other subjects.

In those days, whenever I read Reader's Digest monthly publications, there used to be one article on: "The Most Unforgettable Character" and I loved to eagerly read these articles that I came across. For me, my most unforgettable teacher at the Institute of Economics was Sayar Gyi U Aye Hlaing.

He was the first Rector of the Institute of Economics.

I remember that he came to school driving his black Hillman car. He dressed simply but elegantly. Although we would see him in the important events of the school such as freshers' welcomes, convocations, etc. he did not teach me until I was an under-graduate student doing my masters degree.

His classes were in the Room just beside his office.

And he seemed to enjoy teaching us despite his heavy duties as a Rector.

He would be very prompt walking into the class carrying a bundle of books and slightly throwing them onto the table before beginning the class.

He used to ask us questions at the very beginning or during the class and he would smile while listening to our answers or at the end of our answer and gave his comments and remarks, and carry on with his lecture.

His lectures used to be very powerful in the sense that one would learn a lot of concepts and ideas which would be remembered always.

In the first year of our masters class he taught us Economic and Social Statistics with practical applications in our country, and we learned about the census and how it is collected among other things. In this class we were also joined by masters students from the Statistics Department and so there were about 10 students.

After the first year master's class, I was appointed as a tutor in May1971 at the Department of Economics. I had to wait for one or two years to resume my master I was happy as I could be sitting together in one room with Ko Kyee Myint, myself, Ko Than Htay, Ko Maung Maung Lwin and Ko Than Aung Yin (in that order of sitting – from left to right - while I sat between Ko Kyee Myint and Ko Than Htay).

What I think was the most useful to me later was U Aye Hlaing's teaching to us about pure economic theories and concepts.

The best classes in Economic Theory at the Institute of Economics were the two classes by Dr. U Aye Hlaing in our second year master's class. He taught the History of Economic Thought and Growth Models.

His lectures on Physiocracy, Mercantilism, Classical Economists like Adam Smith, David Ricardo and Karl Marx were among the best.

I also remember his teaching us about production and distribution and specialization and the division of labor.

Growth Models was a subject full of rigorous analyses and equations.

I think Sayar Gyi U Aye Hlaing started with the Harrod-Domar model and its basic equation. Then, he continued with Solow's Growth Model and all the details of steady-state equilibrium.

Eventually, we passed the second year master's class and, the time for our master's thesis came.

When I got my bachelors' degree it was 1969, which coincided with the first year when the first Nobel Prize for Economics was established and awarded.

Jan Tinbergen from the Netherlands School of Economics and Ragnar Frisch of Oslo University received the Nobel Prize for their contributions in Economics.

Automatically, most of us were obsessed with econometrics.

The second economist to receive the Nobel Prize in Economics was Paul A. Samuelson of Massachusetts Institute of Technology.[xiv]

Paul Samuelson's Economics textbook was one of the most used reference books on economics at the school.

Because of their influence on us, we were sort of crazy with mathematical economics and econometrics.

Another towering economist at that time was Chicago School's Milton Friedman, who was famous side by side with Paul Samuelson

The title chosen for my master's thesis was A Monetary Analysis of Burma.

When I formally presented the outline of my thesis to my teachers I was somewhat grilled.

I was asked all the details of my outline, and why I wanted to attempt an ambitious thesis.

Finally, Sayar Gyi U Aye Hlaing came to my rescue. "We should give him a chance to try" were his words, and there was no one who could argue with him.

Another teacher who closely helped me to get my master degree within a short time was Sayar U Myat Thein.

He was one of the lecturers at the Institute of Economics.

Dr. Myo Nyunt was another lecturer who was also close to the students as well as to young tutors like us. His class on mathematical economics was also another subject that we admired. Another lecturer was Dr U Myint, who though from the Institute of Education visited our school very often.

His lecture to the graduate students on mathematical statistics was another class that I enjoyed very much.

It was Sayar U Myat Thein who supervised my master's thesis, and he over-hauled my outline completely dividing it into two parts.

He also advised me to add another chapter on inflation.

Using this chapter we submitted and presented a paper on "Inflation in Burma" at the Burma Research Congress.

He was a hall warden at Ohn Daw Men's Dormitory, and I went there almost every day after work to work on my thesis.

Sayar was very generous.

I was treated as if I was one member of his family.

I think the defense of my thesis was sort of smooth sailing with U Myat Thein as my supervisor.

And so I got my Master of Economics degree in 1975.

*

Then one morning in early 1976, I was called by Dr. U Aye Hlaing to his office.

It was unusual for a tutor to be called by our Rector.

When I sat in front of him at his desk, he said one official from the Ministry of Finance came to him requesting someone from the Department of Economics to join the Ministry as an Assistant Director.

Because I had just obtained my master's degree, he recommended my name.

It was like a promotion.

At that time, a tutor should have a minimum seven years' service to be considered for an Assistant Lecturer position.

There were very little scholarship opportunities to study abroad.

And many had to go mostly to Socialist countries like the Soviet Union, Poland and Czechoslovakia[xv].

When I came back to my office after hearing about the offer from the Finance Ministry, all my colleagues suggested that I should grab this rare opportunity.

Thus, the time arrived for me to say goodbye to the school where I first thought I would teach forever.

I knew that Sayar Gyi U Aye Hlaing did the best for me.

Later I had a privilege to work together with Sayar Gyi U Aye Hlaing again at the Ministry as he became Chairman of the Central Bank.

Dr. U Shein was the Deputy Minister of the Ministry of Planning and Finance.

Sayar Gyi was the trusted professional of the Deputy Minister.

He came to the Ministry almost every day until he retired from the service.

Hla Phyu Chit--2014

Biography of Hla Phyu Chit

Hla Phyu Chit studied at the Institute of Economics, Rangoon from 1965 to 1969; obtained a Bachelor of Economics Degree in Planning and Development. While working on his Masters, he was appointed a tutor at the Economics Department, Institute of Economics in May 1971. He received his M. Econ. in 1975.

Together with his Master's Thesis Supervisor U Myat Thein, he submitted a paper Inflation in Burma at the Burma Research Congress.

In 1976 he was directly recruited by the Ministry of Planning and Finance as Budget Officer, later the Assistant Director until 1987.

He joined the UN Development Project Country Office in Rangoon in May 1987 as Program Officer, later as Program Manager.

In May to August 1993 he was awarded a Research Fellowship at Nagoya School of Economics, Nagoya University. His research paper was A Search for Growth: A Development Management Approach for Myanmar.

In 1995-1996 he studied at the Kennedy School of Government, Harvard University for MPA as a Mason Fellow.

Back to UNDP Yangon, Hla Phyu Chit back-stopped micro-credit/microfinance and poverty survey/assessment programs to pioneer in Myanmar. In 2004, he worked as a Policy Specialist at UNDP/UNOPS Regional Program of Macroeconomics of Poverty Reduction, in Nepal and in Sri Lanka up to 2006.

He resumed his career at UNDP Yangon as Assistant Resident Representative (Program) until he retired in January 2008.

From November 2009 to February 2010 he was recruited by UNOPS Regional Office, Bangkok as an Evaluation Expert. He joined UNOPS Yangon Office in April 2010 as a Human Resources Consultant and later became a Project Support Officer at Global Fund Project to Fight AIDS, TB and Malaria; until June 2013.

In June 2013, he went to the USA and currently he is working as an Independent Contractor for two US Companies.

Hla Phyu Chit has contributed articles and translated short stories in Myanmar Journals and Magazines under the pen name Maung Pye Aung.

LAST CALL FOR IOE MEMORIAL EDITION AND ACKNOWLEDGEMENTS.

Around Dec. 2014, I asked several Contributors to clarify some items, to date no one has responded.

Only about half sent their professional bios to use with the essays.

As you are all adult, even senior, well-trained professionals, I shall not ask you again.

I am going to do the best I can and get it through to press in a few days.

Thank you for writing, and I hope you will continue to support the project by buying the Compilation.

I myself find it informative as well as entertaining to read the essays and find out things I did not know before.

We were all divided and flung around the world by the Burmese Diaspora and political events.

That we can get together electronically to work on this project is a testament to the human spirit, as they say, and also to Facebook and email.

I really must thank Daw Khin Pwint Oo who did 99% of the liaison. Also Roland Khin.

Thank you, Ma Pwint.

mmkmkaung

Facebook 6-18-2015

Appendix1—

Fair warning--for Institute of Economics co-contributors.

I know most of you wrote mostly pleasant things, about your memories of Institute of Economics, Rangoon, 1962-1988.

However, one artist whom I greatly admire, Zaw Win Pe, said in connection with his own work:

"I like to paint in light and bright colors and dark colors and shadow as I think it is more true."

Well, I feel the same about this collection of articles.

If I wanted to gild in garish gold, I would just have told you to send your piece to the official Yangon edition.

Some of you even used the em word, which I may or may not take out.

However, the whole point of having an alternative edition is so it's truer and more balanced.

That means bad impressions or memories will be in it as well as the good.

So I decided I am going to write a hard-hitting piece after all.

And I do think the Inst declined after Dr Findlay and Dr Aye Hlaing left, and like Saya I will illustrate with examples why.

And it was also confirmed to me by an office co-worker downstairs in the office, to whom I went when I was promoted to lecturer in 1978.

It was not someone I knew, or someone I knew well, and I do not remember his name.

However, I found out that my post had a lien on it from a former colleague who went to work at the BSPP party, and it said that should this man come back, I would need to vacate my post for him.

After he saw my expression, this man in the office records section said thoughtfully as if to himself, "It is not like when your Saya Dr. Findlay was here, you know. He wrote you a really good recommendation letter." (for my Asst. Lecturer post?) "It's not like that anymore." (Later, my immigration lawyer would use almost the same words, and Saya also recommended me for my research job at The Burma Fund).

*

That was the first I heard of the lien. Also the then Rector at one time, assigned me to do the accounts for the co-op loans, without consulting me first. I had no trouble there, but still, I don't think it was right, when there were a lot of accountants in the building in the Commerce section.

And I really have no interest in accounting.

My mother however was blasé about it all, "Well, these things they assign someone who has money already, as they know you won't filch anything."

Anyway, all I want to say is in my own article, a lot of darkness will come out.

That's all.

KMKaung

10-17-2014

- . . . and . . . like this.

- Sean Turnell: I know I have said this before Kyi May Kaung - but it is a great and good thing you are doing!

  Unlike · 1

- Kyi May Kaung : Thank you Sean Turnell for your great and abiding support, it means a lot to me. My co-editors have also said that they like my writing style. I will try and keep it as toned down as I can, but, anyway, I think shadows have to be described too.

Appendix 2.

As an editor what I find annoying:

jumpy formatting with no logic

wrong spellings

single-spaced lines

no para indents

idiosyncratic spelling and capitalization, some words in bold, I don't know why

writing about the past in the present tense

a too humble Burmese approach

long unclear sentences—I wish I had not agreed to U Hla Hpyu Chit's request to edit this IER essay collection, but now some of the essays are here, and as I promised, I have to do it.

Not one of the contributors responded to my editorial comments and no one re-formatted their work properly for me—but I don't want something going out under my name to be an infernal mess, so I am spending an unholy amount of time on this.

but I do warn you, since I expect zero sales for an essay collection, all contributors etc. will need to buy your own copy from Amazon, as I will too.

If it's not a labor of love, it is one of annoyance and duty.

But I feel what you wrote deserves an audience, even though some of it is too sentimental for my taste, too sugary, and some, well, I don't know—too sweet—too selective in what you remember (and what you “forget”).

Kyi May Kaung

3-1-2015

Facebook post

Appendix 3

A Thought on All This

by Kyi May Kaung

Like the two famous jazz musicians who told me what they play is not jazz anymore, it is a mix of international and ethnic and . . . what I write is not "Burmese colonial English" any more, and what I cook is not Burmese anymore either.

it is international and fusion—

and as for painting, why should I keep painting Burmese landscapes and Burmese dancers and pagodas—

perhaps to sell, but I do not live and work in Burma.

And anyway, I cannot go back into my old shell, it does not fit anymore.

KMKaung 3-1-2015 Facebook post.

KMKaung, ed. Let It fly with the Flowers: Essays about the Institute of Economics, Rangoon, Burma.

Appendix 4—CV of the Editor—

KYI MAY KAUNG (Ph.D.)

Curriculum Vitae

Website: www.kmkaung.com

Blog: http://kyimaykaung.blogspot.com

Twitter: https://twitter.com/KyiKaung

FaceBook: https://www.facebook.com/kyi.m.kaung

Objective: Position in political and economic analyses, writing, research.

Strong economics and finance background. Consultancy. Excellent at conceptualizing and implementing, macro-economic and systemic views.

Progressive views, wide range of interests.

Excellent writer, meticulous editor.

- Ivy League doctorate in Political Economy.
- Passionately interested in social justice issues.
- Twenty years non-profit experience in the Washington, DC area.
- Twenty years teaching and research experience.
- Able to strategize and set up new organizations.
- Able to speak and write persuasively so people listen.

- Excellent oral and written presentations. Convincing, engaging and experienced public speaker. Fluent English and Burmese. Reading knowledge of French. Willing to learn Mandarin.
- Extensive contacts in the arts, media, academia, Washington DC. Likeable personality.
- Strengths: Fast and accurate boil down of important issues to easily understandable points.• Able to travel domestically and internationally up to 25% of the year.
- Able to formulate strategy and analyze organizational structure and goals.
- Able to formulate and carry out P.R. initiatives.

EDUCATION

Ph.D. City and Regional Planning and Political Science, University of Pennsylvania, May 1994.

M.A. City and Regional Planning, University of Pennsylvania, 1987.

M.A. Economics, University of Rangoon, 1967.

B.A. Honors, Economics, University of Rangoon, 1964.

PUBLICATIONS (Fiction) since 2014

Black Rice—A Novella

The Rider of Crocodiles—A Novella

FGM—A Novella

The Lovers—A Novella

Dancing like a Peacock & Koel Bird—Stories

Band of Flesh and 53 Red Roses—Stories

Home is Where, Housewarming and My Potsdam—Stories

No Crib for a Bed & Other Stories—

AWARDS AND HONORS

Angelina Pedroso Center, NEIU Chicago, 12 April 2012. Award for Service to Asian-American Heritage Festival and for commitment to social change.

http://theofficialpageof.com/northeastern-illinois-university/

My Asian Survey article cited in Burma after 1962: A Failure in Development.

My question of Sen. Jim Webb – why he did not have Burmese Exile Government and other stakeholders at his Hearing in Sept. 09, picked up by Christianne Amanpour in her interview of Exile Government representative Dr. Thaung Htun. Oct. 2009.

My Open Letter/Statement about Webb's Hearing picked up the same day by Jotman and other prominent Burma bloggers, Sept. 2009.

Mention on Poet's Path, Museum of American Poetics, "Asian Verse Beings" page with Thich Hnat Hanh, Maxine Hong Kingston, Ishle Yi Park, Wang Ping and others.

My article on Nargis Cyclone and Burma – picked up by Anderson Cooper Boxxet.

http://www.boxxet.com/Anderson_Cooper/Nargis_Cyclone_and_Burma_by _Kyi_May_Kaung.1srad7.d

Northeastern Illinois University, Distinguished Service Award, for Outstanding Dedication and Work promoting Peace and Democracy in Burma, April 3, 2008.

IMPACTSilverSpring Award, won by Space 7-10 where my Dr. Kaung's Salon is located. 2007

Short List – Earth Rights International PR position 2005 based in Chiangmai, Thailand.

Short List—teaching Multicultural Creative Writing—at Payap University, Chiangmai, Thailand.

Best short story "Black Rice" and best art entry – Painting Mars Ranger – March 2007, The Northern Virginia Review.

William Carlos Williams Award, Academy of American Poets, 1995.

Pennsylvania Council on the Arts Award, for concept for play FLASHBACK (now titled Shaman.)

Pew Finalist, 1996 and 1994, for play SHAMAN and allegory She-Monkey respectively.

Fulbright Scholar, 1982-89. University of Pennsylvania.

HAVE BEEN INTERVIEWED BY:

On Burma, most recently –

Dr. Sean Turnell, Sept. 2014, on my contributions to Burmese Economic Thought, on which he is writing a book.

Patrick Barta of Wall Street Journal interviewed me about reopening Rangoon University, 2012.

Michelle Chen of Asia Pacific Forum interviewed me about change in Burma, is it real. Dec 13th, 2011

http://www.asiapacificforum.org/show-detail.php?show_id=250

October 2011 Kyaw Aung Lwin of VOA interviewed me about poetry reading in front of Burmese embassy DC – 10,000 poets for change.

Burmese Women's Union based in Chiangmai. Thailand on Burma and upcoming so-called 2010 "election" -- Dec. 2009

RFA – on Mirca panel Freedom and Art, in honor of Aung San Suu Kyi. Jan. 2009.

On the role of the younger generation and NGOs in Nargis Cyclone recovery programs. Radio Free Asia -- BUR-2008-0612-2030

Advocate Radio, Westchester, New York -- http://advocates-wvox.com/rss2.aspx

During the 2007 Saffron Revolution.

Canadian Broadcasting Corporation, BBC, National Public Radio; Asian Fortune (Ying Ju Lai); Dr. Michael Hurd Show; Montgomery County TV, Art Scene Channel 16 Lila Snow, Artist; Gazette Newspaper (Audrey Dutton); Silver Spring MD Impact Awards; Boulder Alternative Radio; Kalamazoo Gazette; Boulder Current; Wild River Review; Anil Mundra (now with NPR); Eliot Pfanstiehl, Montgomery County MD TV.

VOLUNTEER POSITIONS

Amnesty International Human Rights Festival, participating artist and presenter, April, MD. 2010.

Co-Host. Coffee klatsch for those who work at home, Busboys and Poets, DC. Aug 08 - 2009-Nov 2009.

Supporter – U.S. Campaign for Burma.

Co-founder, founding board member – VAHU. A think tank without walls for Burma. We teach Burmese from inside Burma how to write winning project proposals.

Founder/facilitator/presenter: Dr. Kaung's Salon and Dr. Kaung's Bookshelf, 963 Bonifant St. Silver Spring, MD.

Dr. Kaung's Salon from Oct 2005-2009 – some highlights:

Burma and Haiti: Dictators, Disasters and International Aid, Silver Spring, MD. 4-9-2010

Wizard of the Crow, by Ngugi Thiong'o, A Survey of Books on Cambodia, Pakistan and Benazir Bhutto. Monologue as a hysterectomy victim. Book discussion -- Beasts of No Nation, by Uzodinma Iweala. Robin Hood Ballads by Dr. Stephen Winick, Discussion of Nobel prize winning writer Orhan Pamuk, James Frey's A Million Little Pieces, book launches by Meena Nayak, artist Lila Snow, journalist Melissa Robinson, architect Werner Krebs on stage design, Eniko Basa on The 1956 Hungarian Revolution, dancers Martha Wittman and Elizabeth Johnson choreographing immigrant stories, Elizabeth Null folk sing, Christmas Carol Sing, Bijan C. Bayne and Tomiko Anders on "Who am I?" Dancer Gretchen Dunn performing placeDISplace.

Member, Speculative Fiction Group (363 members)—Meetup, DC, Sept 2014--

Member, FBB – Friday Brunch Group – networking for writers with Nita Congress, August 2007-

Co-founder, Member, Writing Group, WRITE ON, DC. August 2005 – Sept. 2006

Co-founder, Writing Group, The East-West Group, MD, April 2005 - Oct. 2005

Member, Washington Independent Writers, Travel Writers' Group, 2006 – 2007.

Board member, Burma Refugee Project, (medical aid to refugees), Jan 2005-July 2011

Board Member, Burma Economic Watch, An Electronic Magazine, Macquarie University, Sydney, Australia. 2004 to present.

Member, Technical Advisory Network, Burmese Government in Exile, 2000-present.

EMPLOYMENT

Free Lance Writer, Consultant, Analyst and Visual Artist.

Sept. 21, 2011-

Free lance blogger/columnist for Asian Correspondent.

Dec. 1, 2008 – May 2009.

Program Assistant/Coordinator, Independent Diplomat, Washington D.C. and National Coalition Government of the Union of Burma, Rockville, MD.

Link to major Plan for Democracy and Development that I wrote (compiled) for the Exile Government.

http://www.ncgub.net/NCGUB/mediagallery/download85d1.pdf?mid=20091023154306771

Private Consultant – 2004-

2006- VAHU co-founder and Sr. Analyst.

2005- Consultant and Free Lance Writer. Professional artist.

Senior Research Associate. The Burma Fund, Washington DC, Sept 2001-Dec 31, 2004

Senior Research Analyst. Radio Free Asia, Washington DC, May 1998-Sept 2001.

International Radio Broadcaster, RFA Burmese Service, Washington DC, March 1997-April 1998.

Ph.D. candidate, University of Pennsylvania, Philadelphia.

1978-1988. Assoc. Professor, Economics Department, University of Rangoon, Burma

SEMINARS/CONFERENCES, STRATEGIZING SESSIONS 2001 – PRESENT.

September 2012, Columbia University Rohingya Conference, keynote speaker A.K. Sen--helped invite 50% of the 12 member panel.

April 12, 2012, So-called Reforms in Burma.

Angelina Pedroso Center, NEIU, Chicago.

Poetry reading in front of Burmese Embassy, DC. 100,000 Poets for Change.

http://www.100tpcmedia.org/washingtondc/burma-kyi_may_kaung_2.html

March 10-11th, 2011, NEIU, Chicago.

Two panels:

Prospects for non-violent change in Burma and Iran.

Gandhi's principles of non-violence, Aung San Suu Kyi and Burma.

http://www.neiu.edu/~cdia/Non-Violence_Peace_Conference_files/Preliminary%20Program.pdf

Dec 2010, Article in PeacexPeace – The Recent Release of Aung San Suu Kyi: A Cynical Ploy. On line publication

Sept 28, 2010, Payap University, Chiangmai,Thailand –

Burma 2010: Sham Elections as Expected

http://ic.payap.ac.th/index.php?cal=cal&month=9&year=2010

Northeastern IL Univ., March 31, 2010. Planning Committee for Annual Asian-Heritage Festival.

Panelist. Burma and Iran: Elections, Democracy and Human Rights. With Dr. Hamid Al Akbari, 3-31-2010, NEIU, Chicago.

Article in Opinion Asia, 2009.

Mirca Art Group, Beacon, NY. Art for Freedom and Aung San Suu Kyi. Panelist. Feb 14, 2009. http://www.amnestyusa.org/print.php

http://www.artslant.com/global/artists/show/52745-mirca-art-group-travelling-shows

http://www.mirca-art.com/Panel2%5B1%5D.pdf

http://www.mizzima.com/archive/1689-international-artists-launch-awareness-drive-for-aung-san-suu-kyi.html

Panel on Peace Mural, Georgetown, Washington DC, Jan 28, 2009. Sponsored by Institute for Policy Studies.

Nov. 2008, Read non-profit employees' from inside Burma's project proposals and action plans and chose three winning proposals for cash prizes from CDCE, Chiangmai, Thailand.

Oct 3-5, 2008. Burma Studies Group, "What's wrong with Burma Studies? An overview since 1988."

June 12, 2008. E-W Center, Washington DC. Panelist. Strategizing after Cyclone Nargis in Burma.

http://www.eastwestcenter.org/index.php?id=3631&print=1

June 6-10, 2008. Presenter and moderator, Forum of Burmese in Europe, Helsinki, Finland. Hosted by Finnish Foreign Ministry.

March, 2008. Presenter/Awardee. Session on Burma, India and China, Northeastern Illinois University, Chicago.

http://www.neiu.edu/DOCUMENTS/Home%20-%20Docs/Asian_Program_08.pdf

Asian American Heritage Festival, National Autonomy, Examining the 60th Anniversary

of Burma and India's Independence, Hon. Ashok Kumar Attri, Consul General of India, Chicago, and Kyi May Kaung, artist and poet, Burmese activist. Moderated by Hamid Akbari, Chair and Associate Professor, Management and Marketing, NEIU.

Jan. 24, 2008. Strategizing meeting for Burma activism. Woman's National Demcratic Club, D.C.

http://www.burmanet.org/news/2007/12/05/mizzima-news-post-crisis-economic-fallout-in-burma-kyi-may-kaung/

May 12, 2007, Post crisis economic fallout in Burma, in Mizzima on line. Accessed 7-18-2011

Oct 19, 2007. Panelist. Burma- Post Clampdown, What is to be Done? American University, School of International Studies.

April 27, 2007. Panelist on Education and Generational Change. Burma Youth Project, American University, Washington, DC.

April 5, 2007, Northeastern Illinois University, Focus on Burma and Aung San Suu Kyi – On the keynote panel.

Dec. 2006, Chiangmai University, Community Development Project. Read course attendees project paper proposals and chose winning team.

November 2006, Refugee Conference – American University – one of invited speakers.

October- Dec., 2006. Refugee art exhibit, one of invited painters. Helped plan the exhibition, Gateway Heliport Gallery, Silver Spring, MD.

July 2006, E-W Center D.C. sponsored a closed-door conference on Conflict Resolution in Burma in Bangkok. I was one of a dozen invited commentators/rapporteurs.

http://www.eastwestcenter.org/index.php?id=4641&print=1

July 2006, Burma Studies Group – Singapore.

2005- Co-founder, founding board member (with Zaw Oo) of VAHU/CDCE which trains non-profit workers from Burma.

October 2005, The Politics of Voices, House of World Culture, Berlin. Invited with 5 other S.E. Asian writers "who dare to confront."

http://www.hkw.de/en/ressourcen/archiv2005/raeumeundschatten/veranstaltung_1343/Veranstaltungsdetail_1_5313.php

Nov. 2002. SAIS, Johns Hopkins, Washington DC. Participant. Strategizing for Burmese democracy movement in exile.

Sept, 2002. Burma Studies Conference, Gottenberg, Sweden, co-chaired panel on Diplomacy and Dialog in Burma.

Jan. 2003, Conference on Forced Migration and Burma, Chiangmai, Thaíland.

July 2003, Canberra, Australia, Australian National University, Peer Reviewed book on Economic Transitions in Burma. Peers from Burmese Democratic Government in Exile,

July 2003, Sydney, Australia, Australia Burmese Students Conference.

March 2003, Globalization and Human Trafficking, Denver CO.

Aug. 2002, International IDEA Stockholm, Democratic Capacity Building for Burma.

Aug 2002, Burma Studies Conference, co-chair – keynote panel Democracy and Dialog in Burma.

http://www.paclii.org/journals/fJSPL/vol07no1/1.shtml

August 2002, Asean People's Assembly, "Globalisation and ASEAN," Bali, Indonesia.

April 2001 Conference on World Affairs, Boulder CO. "World without Borders."

1997-2001 – annual Conferences on World Affairs, poetry, visual art, presentations on Burma.

April 1995 – with Dr Silverstein in Alberta, Canada, Burma into the 21st Century – Canadian Friends of Burma.

ftp://sunsite.unc.edu/pub/academic/political-science/freeburma/ba/1995/ba0595.html

1994, University of Toronto, Canada, Canadian Friends of Burma – panel whether to boycott Tourism Year in Burma.

Interviewed on Burma by:

VOA 9-24-2011 – on my poetry reading Poems in a Plastic Bag, in front of Myanmar Embassy DC with Split this Rock, Sarah Browning.

VOA TV, Sept 2009, on my art show Identity, Mostly Burmese Monks.

By Peace by Peace, Sept 2009, on my life as a dissident.

Interviewed by RFA – Art for Suu Kyi, Feb 15, 2009. Five minute piece broadcast 2-17-09 – 7 AM Burma Standard Time.

Radio Free Asia, June 12, 2008 on lack of legitimacy of Burmese junta, especially after Cyclone Nargis. BUR-2008-0612-2030

May 21st, 2008 – Richard Garfunkel of The Advocate Radio – New Rochelle New York, on the political effects of Cyclone Nargis in Burma.

http://advocates-wvox.com/2008/05/21/burma-human-tragedy-and-social-disaster-45-years-in-the-making.aspx

Jan 1, 2008 RFA, "Burma's Economic Prospects in 2008."

September 2007 Burmese Monks' Crisis

1. BBC (World) HardTalk --

http://news.bbc.co.uk/2/hi/programmes/hardtalk/7026645.stm

2. KALW San Francisco Radio – Your Call with Rose Aguiler

http://yourcallradio.blogspot.com/

3. CBC – with Suhana Meharchand in Toronto –Sept. 24th, 2007 – in which I correctly predicted that the clampdown would happen in the next 24 hours.

October 4, 2007 – post-clampdown analysis –

4. Ask Hugh (Williamson) – radio out of Berkeley, CA.

5. CapeTown Voice – Jihad Omar – On Burmese Monks' Saffron Revolution.

2001- 2007:

Canadian Broadcasting Corporation; National Public Radio; Voice of America Burmese Service and Talk to America; Pacifica Radio; Radio Free Asia; Asian Fortune (Ying Ju Lai); Dr. Michael Hurd Show; Montgomery County TV, Art Scene Channel 16 Lila Snow, Artist; Gazette Newspaper (Audrey Dutton); Silver Spring MD Impact Awards; Boulder Alternative Radio; Kalamazoo Gazette; Boulder Current; Wild River Review; Anil Mundra; Eliot Pfanstiehl.

LATEST PUBLICATIONS AND PRESENTATIONS (Partial List)

Since 2013--

Eight novellas and short story collections—available on Amazon.com

Black Rice

FGM

Rider of Crocodiles

The Lovers

Dancing like a Peacock, Koel Bird: Stories from the Burma-Thai Border

No Crib for a Bed: Immigrant Stories.

Asian Correspondent – columnist.

Satire, fiction, creative non-fiction: A Burmese Vampire Story – on scramble for Burma's resources.

http://asiancorrespondent.com/author/kyimaykaung/

Dec 1, 2011. Himal Southasia cover feature-

http://www.himalmag.com/component/content/article/4842-potemkin-politics.html

Potemkin politics: Are Burmese reforms for real? Print and on line editions.

Oct 24, 2011. Poetry reading in front of Burmese embassy DC on PeacexPeace.

Oct 14, 2011 – on Asian Correspondent –

http://asiancorrespondent.com/67276/zarganar-or-pincers-great-burmese-comic-among-few-released/

Mentioned in Sarah Browning's article on Poetry Walk of Shame in Foreign Policy in Focus.

http://www.fpif.org/articles/poets_stand_up

Oct 12, 2011. Poem War Against Roaches in Foreign Policy in Focus.

http://www.fpif.org/articles/war_on_roaches

Poem--War on Roaches in Counterpunch--

http://www.counterpunch.org/2011/09/09/jared-carter-and-kyi-may-kaung/

Sept. 24 – 2011 Poetry readings in front of Burmese, Yemen embassies, etc. Washington, DC, DC Poets Against War.

http://washingtonexaminer.com/local/people/2011/09/3-minute-interview-sarah-browning

Sept. 21, 2011 – first blog column on Asian Correspondent, "VOA inside Burma: In a white suit like Christianne Amanpour".

Sept., 2011 my poem War on Roaches in Poets' Basement, Counterpunch.

Painting Shan Black Belt Saves the World or Running Leap –

Space 7-10 Alumni potluck show, Aug 9-Sept 3, 2011, Silver Spring, MD.

Aung San Suu Kyi's Role – July 2011

http://www.morungexpress.com/analysis/30616.html

January 6, 2011 PeacexPeace The Recent Release of Aung San Suu Kyi: A Cynical Ploy? By Kyi May Kaung http://www.peacexpeace.org/2011/01/the-recent-release-of-aung-san-suu-kyi-a-cynical-ploy/

My blogs http://kyimaykaung.blogspot.com

Kyi Kaung @ Red Room.

Free Aung San Suu Kyi and Burma Blog.

Book Review, U Win Tin's (of Burma's National League for Democracy) prison memoir, What's That? A Human Hell. Foreign Policy in Focus, April 2010.

http://www.fpif.org/articles/review_whats_that_a_human_hell

http://www.eurasiareview.com/2010/05/review-whats-that-human-hell

www.truthout.org

Amnesty International Human Rights Festival, participating artist and presenter.

Exhibited portrait of Aung San Suu Kyi at Space 7-10 Silver Spring, MD.

Presentations, Burma and Human Rights Abuses and "Election" April 24, 2010, Taste of Jerusalem, Silver Spring, MD.

Poetry Reading, Pelted with Petals, the Burmese poems, Nicaros, April 25, 2010, Silver Spring, MD.

September 2009, Identity: Mostly Burmese Monks, paintings exhibited at Space 7-10, Silver Spring, MD.

http://www.artsdc.com/archive/archiveseptember09.html

Poem, Death of Neda, in Asian-American Poetry on line. Dec. 2009.

Article: Burma-Aung San Suu Kyi Verdict and Yettaw- Back to Square One?

http://opinionasia.com/ASSKYettaw

Article: Back to Square One?

http://www.gulfnews.com/opinion/columns/world/10342780.html

Comment on Sen. Webb in Burma, World Tribune,

http://www.worldtribune.com/worldtribune/WTARC/2009/mz0667_08_14.asp

Article- Burma and Ban Ki-moon: The end game? UPI Asia International on line

July 8, 2009.

http://www.upiasia.com/Politics/2009/07/08/burma_and_ban_ki-moon_the_end_game/6956/

May 2009, American University, Burmese Faces, painting exhibition.

Panelist- War and Remembering, Institute of Policy Studies, Feb. 2009.

Friendship Heights Village Center, Cut and Paste, collage show. Sept 2008.

http://www.friendshipheightsmd.gov/PDFs/Sep08NwslttrFINAL.pdf

Profile of Vietnamese artist Huong and her Peace Mural Project, FPIF, Dec. 2008.

Book Review of Joseph Stiglitz and Linda Bilmes' The Three Trillion Dollar War, for Foreign Policy in Focus, Nov. 2008.

Burma: Waiting for the Dawn, in OpenDemocracy, 8-8-2008

For 20th Anniversary of Burma's 8-8-1988 uprising.

Two poems in Counterpunch.

One poem in Napalm Health Spa.

Two poems in Glass Poetry Journal http://glass-poetry0101.blogspot.com/ May 31, 2008.

Two poems in Language for a New Century, W.W. Norton, March 2008.

One poem in Amnesty International and the New Republic's Fire in the Soul.

Burma: The Great Storm that Changed it All? Wild River Review at Large – May 9, 2008

Interviewed by The Advocates, NY based radio –

http://advocates-wvox.com/2008/05/21/burma-human-tragedy-and-social-disaster-45-years-in-the-making.aspx

Panel discussions: Burma and India, 60 years after Independence. April 2, 2008

Prospects for Peace and Democracy in Burma, April 3, 2008 – NEIU, Chicago, 13th Annual Asian American Festival.

"All about Cambodia" A literature survey type discussion on books about Cambodia. Dr. Kaung's Bookshelf, March 28, Silver Spring, MD.

Burma: Post Clampdown, What should be done? Presentation at Payap University, Chiangmai, Thailand, Feb. 25, 2008.

Burma: Monks and Democracy, Jan. 24, 2008. Woman's National Democratic Club, Washington DC. (Oral presentation)

Special three-part program on Economic Prospects for Burma, China and India in 2008. Jan 2008. Interviewed by Khin May Zaw of RFA. (This program was praised by economists inside Burma)

Burma: Post Clampdown – What Should be Done? The American Prospect, on line. October 2007.

United States Senate Hearing of Oct. 2, 2007. New Mandala, a publication of Australian National University.

Also on my blog – http://kyimaykaung.blogspot.com

(Oral presentation – International Development Program Student Association, American University – Oct 19, 2007)

In house policy briefs for VAHU Development Institute.

How to Find out the Truth about Burma, paper on primary sources with respect to current crisis. New Mandala (A Publication of Australian National University), Nov. 2007.

October http://kyimaykaung.blogspot.com

Foreign Policy in Focus, Monks vs The Military, Sept. 26, 2007, http://www.fpif.org/fpiftxt/4582

Foreign Policy in Focus, Burma, Growing Darker Daily, 9-11-2007 – on current crisis in Burma.

Foreign Policy in Focus, Out of Burma- on dissident literature in Burma.

Asian Fortune, Obit of U Kyaw Htun, Washington Times Editor.

Asian Fortune, on Vineeta Gupta, Indian AIDS activist.

Asian Fortune Newspaper. May 2007. Articles on Bob James' Jazz and Angels of Shanghai, http://www.asianfortunenews.com/site/article_0507.php?article_id=6

On Hla Ohn Mae, Burmese dissident. www.asianfortune.com

Foreign Policy in Focus. Debate on Sanctions in Burma. Jan. 2007

Wild River Review Blog, Reflections on a Begging Bowl: Monks Demonstrate in Burma. Sept 26, 2007.

Wild River Review – Burmese Migrant Workers and Shrimp Shelling and Tuna Canning in Mahachai, Thailand – March14, 2007.

Also in Burma Economic Watch, on line.

Wild River Review – fiction

Short story – The Lovers.

http://www.wildriverreview.com/2/2-shortstories_lovers.html

Wild River Review – profile of Eritrean artist Elsa Gebreyesus

http://www.wildriverreview.com/2/2-profiles_gebreyesus.html

vol. 2, #2, c. 2005

OpenDemocracy articles. 2006-2007

Asian Survey

The Irrawaddy (Burmese dissident magazine – read by members of Congress)

Launched Nov. 2, 2007 – Dr. Kaung's Book Shelf – a series of book discussions – at Space 710, Silver Spring, MD.

Co-founded – **VAHU** Development Institute, a think tank without walls, for Burma, 2005. Over the recent Burma crisis in 2007, VAHU analysts were interviewed a total of 120 times. We have trained 90 monks and 130 civilian non-profit workers in batches. Since 2011, I am no longer with them nor with CDCE (Community Development and Civic Engagement) based in Chiangmai, Thailand.

[i] Editor's note—Just before they left, Dr. Maung Shein and his wife Mrs. Shein lost an infant baby shortly after birth. I went to the house, and still remember the tiny child laid out. As I also lost a baby niece at around this time in similar circumstances, I will always remember this unnecessary death also, a byproduct of Burma's colossally failed economy. KMK

[ii] Of course, Saya Shein was in class, composed of both men and women, and maybe he was trying to be humorous. But the real reason is lack of education and also Ne Win's regime outlawed birth control, allegedly because he wanted a large population to fight wars on the NE border with China. He had a China phobia and a love-hate relationship with China, but I did hear him say in public that he was Chinese and his real name was Shu Maung. KMK.

[iii] In class, Saya Aye Hlaing had a rapid fire gunshot style, with questions going around at the speed of light, in random sequence. He often ignored me sitting up straight with my hand up and looking at him, but would hone in on someone trying to hide, who obviously did not know the answer. I remember one session on Balance of Payments and Unrequited Payments. As my dear classmate MMK struggled to find the answer, Saya said gruffly, "Stop beating around the bush. Get to the point. Did you never hear of unrequited love?" Of course, it was all put on, he was in truth the kindest of humans and he did want us to learn so much. KMK

[iv] Burmese Era.

[v] Transliteration is not standard and hard to read, I asked for re-write but got no response.

[vi] Included with permission.

[vii] Ma Ma means Elder Sister.

[viii] http://en.wikipedia.org/wiki/Syllabary
6-8-2015

[ix] As editor, I must say that all my contributors here come from a more civilized generation before 1988. I am so sad to say it, but many who came out post-1988, the great watershed moment of the failed Burmese Democracy Revolution, learned many bad things from their time under Ne Win, and also their traumas through the jungle. As it would add more "shit" to this compilation, I won't go into all that here. Kmk 6-17-2015

[x] Shawl that all women instructors were required to wear.

[xi] U Hla Phyu Chit is referring to that unhappy phase in IOE history, when Saya Findlay was being "phased out" on account of his

racial origins. I consider it a black mark on the history of the institute. I also mention it in my piece. Dr. Findlay is now Ragnar Nurkse Professor of Economics at Columbia University in New York City, and was there since he emigrated in 1967.

[xii] The Social Science Library set up by the Ford Foundation which donated the building. The founding librarian was Mr. Paul Bixler. As my brother, also a librarian, was a close friend of the Bixlers, Paul and Norma, I visited them in Columbus, Ohio in c. 1983 or 4.

[xiii] Said to have made a living as an astrologer after retiring, but I do not know the details.

[xiv] The mentor of Dr. Ronald Findlay at Massachusetts Institute of Technology, who also told me he was in John Nash (A Beautiful Mind)'s class. Recently, both Dr. John Nash and his wife Mrs. Alicia Nash were killed while in a taxi in a traffic accident on the New Jersey Turnpike near Princeton, New Jersey. They were on their way home to Princeton from Newark Airport after a ceremony in Norway. Kmk

http://nypost.com/2015/05/26/worst-fear-realized-john-nashs-mentally-ill-son-is-now-alone/

6-17-2015

[xv] I myself went to Poland, but returned at the end of an eight month Diploma in Economic Planning course in Warsaw.

www.ingramcontent.com/pod-product-compliance
Lightning Source LLC
Chambersburg PA
CBHW071043290526
45795CB00004B/1295
9781514616376